No Sign
Of A Saint

LARRY DUCE COBB

iUniverse, Inc.
New York Bloomington

No Sign Of A Saint
Poems By: Mr. Larry "Duce" Cobb

iUniverse books may be ordered through booksellers or by contacting:

iUniverse
1663 Liberty Drive
Bloomington, IN 47403
www.iuniverse.com
1-800-Authors (1-800-288-4677)

ISBN: 978-1-4401-9200-5 (sc)
ISBN: 978-1-4401-9201-2 (ebk)

Printed in the United States of America

iUniverse rev. date: 12/17/2009

A Reality
Within each and every
Page of this here book
There lives, absolute truth
And all of what it took
To help find a way out of
The muck and all the mire
As I and others changed course
By stepping away from the fire
Their names weren't used
Only to protect the guilty
Guilty of making a better way,
A reality......

ACKNOWLEDGEMENTS

• First I would like to Thank the one responsible for all that happens in life, Almighty God. Secondly, to the one that gave me life. Mrs. Addie Jane Cobb (Love you Ma) Next I want to express my deepest gratitude to a woman who was, and is there for me, Ms. Mari-Jane Simoneau. Here's a shout out to da hood (Roxbury, Mass). I also would like to give a shout out to my family members and personal friends.(You know who you are). I also thank God for sending me to a place that gave me the opportunity to reach inside of myself and find this ability to write, create and bring to life my poetry.

This is a very special thanks to the late and great Mr. Charlie (Satin Top) Johnson for his help in telling me that I could do this. And to his sister, Ms Joannie Henderson and family. That's just how we do it in Roxbury.

Last but not the least, I give the utmost thanks, respect and gratitude to a very good friend of mine. Mr. Andrew (Yie) Roberts also an author, of a novel called "Dear Mama" This gentleman showed me what, where and how to publish my works. And for that I'm forever grateful. Love Ya Bro!

MR. LARRY "DUCE" COBB BIO

Mr. Larry "Duce" Cobb was born in Covington, Georgia. As a child his family relocated to Boston Massachusetts where life for him as he knew it began. Within life's ups and downs through conversations, he could paint a picture that could be seen and felt. Unbeknownst to him, it was a spring that brought forth the water from the well. Now it is seen and felt within the spoken word through the stories/poems he tells.

He has been writing since 1993. Through the Grace of God, he has performed at many open mike events. Some stage performances and on many and any street corners where there are many listeners. He has recorded a six (6) track CD, as well as a seventeen (17) track CD.

All of this is and was inspired by the words of his loving mother, Ms. Addie J. Cobb. (May God Bless Her Soul) "I can hear her saying, Write a book."

Places he has performed at include; UMass Boston, The opening act for R&B Legends, The Whispers, The Mighty Clouds of Joy at the Cambridge World's Fair, Dennis Edwards and The Temptations Review, The Bowery Poetry Club in New York City for Bruce George, and the BNN Community Access TV Station in Boston Mass.

Artists who have inspired him are: Maya Angelou, Marvin Gaye, Curtis Mayfield, Sam Cooke, James Brown, and Barry White, B.B. King, Bobby Blue Bland and a host of others.

Mr. Cobb was also the winner of the New England Urban Music Awards for Best Male Spoken Word Artist in 2007, 2008.

God gave him a gift so he wants to give to others what God gave to him.

He is also still willing to accept opportunities roxburypoet@yahoo.com

NO SIGN OF A SAINT

As a child amazed
By what I saw
While in the playground
Riding on the seesaw
Now I'm a grown man
Still times, I'm in awe
Years come, years go
I've shown many a flaw
Still voices are saying
Boy stop that playing
You gotta start living
To GOD, you better be praying
Beyond playground I went
Life on high, high, down it went
Thank GOD, death didn't come on pavement
Angels were there heave sent
My, my, my, cry, cry, cry
B.B. King told no lie
Running with crew, street gang
I've lived lyrics blues singers sang
What I had, now long gone
How I was living, I saw no wrong
Before that, it was basketball
Winters were spent playing football
Summer was enjoyed playing baseball
Afterward it came, street call
Red alert, red alert
Young life about to hurt
Always chasing a skirt
Here and there, I'd work

Where'd time go
Where'd time go
Does anyone know
Holler, holler if you know
Life's just a blink of the eye
In our youth, we could touch the sky
Tick, tick, tick time goes bye, bye
Think about it my, my, my
Within the playgrounds
Far distant, joyful sound
Of those not here no more
My brother, you're missed to the core
I hear yea, I hear yea, your laughter
That's the stuff we were chasing after
Farewell, farewell
You're still here in stories I tell
May GOD almighty treat you well
Farewell, miss ya can't ya tell
Daily walking streets I pave
Here and there I see your face
Knowing you're R.I.P. in you grave
Within my heart you have a place
Streets we robbed, being drug slaves
Through GOD's mercy and grace I was saved
Got to keep on pushing

Got to keep on pushing
Keep it moving
Keep it moving
Many times old folks said
Mama would say use your head
You can live, or walk around living dead
You know that's real
Reader do you feel
Cold winds may blow
Warmth comes when you know
LIFE'S now a side show
What's next, now you know
Can you show proof
You can live beyond your youth
Time will tell
Otherwise, farewell
LIFE'S picture that we paint
Show no sign of a saint
March 13, 2003

Poem Comments/ Interpretation

Send Your Comments/*Interpretations* to Mr. Larry "Duce" Cobb
email address; roxburypoet@yahoo.com

THOUGHT YOU KNEW

Thought you knew
Your good and bad
Made Mama glad and sad
She believed you could
Always thought you would
Give up bad, for plenty good
Others or own brothers
Gold you got to off with a rip
On the run Mama's baby son
Baby, baby what you done
Watch yourself please don't slip
Mama said, once she was
Caught in the grip, shining star took a dip
Thought you knew
Good belongs to you
To GOD, I pray you make it through
Leave behind troubles you brought
Stand up son, if you ever get caught
Now you're hunted and sought
Son, son, son what you thought
Thought you knew
Mama's tears were for you
She didn't live to see
Dreams of dreams come true
Son, son see what life was done
You've robbed, and stole your joy and fun
Mama, if you could only see
Me looking at the picture

You left behind for me
Saying and praying, Son, Son
Hear the words I speak
Life I pray for you to keep
Knew you thought
Danger was your life style
Wearing a frown, forgotten how to smile
Through your every walked or ran mile
GOD, and Mama been with you all the while
Thought you knew
My Son, My Son
When you didn't love you
Thinking your crew, was true blue
Shit went down, who told on you
Think about it, locked down time you do
Lonely in there, lonely in there
Lights out, lights out
Broken dreams, tears role out
Through the darkness, please understand
There's more and more to being a man
Son, Son, Son
Hear the words I speak
Life, I pray for you to keep
Thought you knew
Thought you knew
Dec 22, 25 2002

Poem Comments/ Interpretation

_____
_____
_____
_____
_____
_____
_____
_____
_____
_____
_____
_____
_____
_____
_____
_____
_____
_____
_____
_____
_____
_____
_____
_____
_____

Send Your Comments/Interpretations to Mr. Larry "Duce" Cobb
email address; roxburypoet@yahoo.com

SIGNS OF THE TIME

Signs of the times
See the sign
Quite a line
Where it was once kind
Now lives, unemployment
Homelessness, and one more soup line
The rich get richer
Leaving behind poor
Builds more digs deeper the ditch
Here's the electric chair
Some say hit the damn switch
Because living in America today
Is a bitch
Hunger and pain
Locks minds in the constant strain
Good people and good sense
Have a way of going down the drain
Face it eyeball to eyeball
Living beyond it that's gain
Hopes not seen on the block
Because confusion and illusion
Stop the youth on the spot

Curtis Mayfield said it all
Future shock
Dreams come to be broken
God's the only repair shop open
Marvin Gaye what's going on
Politicians keep saying hold on be strong
This shit won't last long
Sam Cooke what more will be taken
After whats been took
Stop listen and look
A change has got to come
Can't you see what's being done
From midnight to the morning sun
What's the problem
Is it genocide oh my God another suicide
Solutions not buck wild homicide
Why cry try hear the future cry
For betterment always try
Because if you give up
Despair does another drive by
Quite a line
See the signs
Signs of the times
August 10, 2003

Poem Comments/ Interpretation

MORE THAN FRIENDS

For every love
That's lost
There's sure to be
One found
I thank GOD
And whom ever lost you
Because I'm so glad
It was you
That I found
Here' something
You need to know
This love for you
Continues to grow
Not as the waterless flower
Shall this ever wilt
The foundation is place
To what GOD's love has built
Understanding, care
Tenderness, and respect
The love we share
It's meant for us to protect
Within my heart

I do believe
Yours is a love
That just won't leave
It's you and you only
You've kept me away
From living my life lonely
You're the shadow
Standing by my side
The love you share
Never-ever seems to hide
From beginning to now
You've kept it in plain view
That's the reason why
My affections belong to you
May the kindness
Of good fortune
Forever ride the winds
For Lady and I
Who've become
MORE THAN FRIENDS
Oct 23, 1998

Poem Comments/ Interpretation

_____
_____
_____
_____
_____
_____
_____
_____
_____
_____
_____
_____
_____
_____
_____
_____
_____
_____
_____
_____
_____
_____
_____

Send Your Comments/_Interpretations_ to Mr. Larry "Duce" Cobb
email address; roxburypoet@yahoo.com

THAT I ONCE DID WRONG

When to the drugs
I turned on
I never imagined
It would last this long
It went from
A why don't you try
To now where I'm
Sending out an outward cry
I robbed Peter to pay Paul
Just for the drugs and that's all
While hustling for the money
I didn't see the world
Fun or funny
Through rain, hail
Sleet and snow
The drugs would say
You know it's time to go
While being out in those streets
If no drugs was in the food
The hell with anything to eat
Cause it constantly
Keeps you on the chase
Only to destroy the life
That you and I waste

Though I wanted to recover
My weakness wouldn't allow me
I've come to discover
My stop started with jail
When the judge
And the bondsmen
Wouldn't grant me bail
This is the history
To each and all
That have a drug history
It's time to find
That life is truly dear
And it all starts here
Strength is in numbers
Wisdom comes when you and I
Become one of the numbers
That I once did wrong
History has shown me
The places I need not be
That's something I won't repeat
Because there's something
Better that I seek
Those were the unproductive years
That I still now
Wipe away the tears

For not reaching for my peak
While spending too much time in the streets
As I chased the infamous
Vanishing dream
Looking back how could I have treated
Myself that dam mean
Yes like the old folk said
You live and learn
If you can manage to survive
Surely you can earn
From what you've learned
Yes very well I was taught this lesion
With help of GOD
And of His timely blessings
To the point I can carry on
Because He bestowed upon me
A will be strong
From all the things
That I once did wrong.
January 24, 1994

Poem Comments/ Interpretation

SINCE THAT DAY

Out of a flock
Of one hundred
I was the lost one
Broken spirit
Hidden in darkness
Removed from the sun
GOD sent a Sheppard
For the likes of me
Guiding me to the light
Only to set me free
Something not to forget
The Temptations song
A day to remember
Theirs was the third
Mine's was the 16th of September
A memorable night
Then it arrived, the light
Desire came to live
GOD had to have known
I have more to give
Thank you GOD
For allowing me to live
Humbling, for a soldier as I

Traveling I've stood
In the house of GOD
There just to cry
Anyone, or anybody saying
That would be me
I would've said their insane
Now understand
The blessing by GOD has no pain
To something, there was an end
When the darkness moved
GOD is still my friend
Leading me in the right way
That's my story
Since that day
April 11, 2002

Poem Comments/ Interpretation

_____
_____
_____
_____
_____
_____
_____
_____
_____
_____
_____
_____
_____
_____
_____
_____
_____
_____
_____
_____
_____
_____
_____
_____
_____

Send Your Comments/Interpretations to Mr. Larry "Duce" Cobb
email address; roxburypoet@yahoo.com

SILENT PRAYER

Stories heard at Mama's feet
Between the cradle to the street
Be careful of what you seek
A broken dream, a lost hope
Saying to the other
Dam just can't cope
Then there's others
Chasing wine, coke, and dope
Within days of many lives
Gun shots, more drive bys
Not one, death took two lives
Alone a Mother cries and cries
Promise came to it's demise
Left behind at the wake
It's heard for GOD sake
What do we do with birthday cake
Another Mother's world is torn apart
While asking GOD
When is stop gonna start
Silent prayer, from a Mother's heart
Silent prayer
Silent prayer
Aug 4, 2004

Poem Comments/
Interpretation

_____
_____
_____
_____
_____
_____
_____
_____
_____
_____
_____
_____
_____
_____
_____
_____
_____
_____
_____
_____
_____
_____
_____
_____

EYES IN WINDOWS

Eyes in windows
We're out here
To those in there
At souls they stare
Without an ounce of care
Seeing a drought no rain living under
Stress and strain
Hunger delivers pain
Out here it's tough to maintain
In there feasting on caviar
Stepping on dreams of dreamers
As they puff on Cuban cigars
Driving by in stretch Cadillac cars
Short stopping prayers
Sent beyond the stars
We're out here to those in there
Homeless, jobless, penniless
These are the seeds
That produce ruthlessness
When hope is taken for success
God knows we're not lifeless
What goes around comers around
Watch well for the bloodhound
Keeper of the torch
How does that sound
That sound
Without an ounce of care
At souls they stare
To those in there
We're out here
Eyes in windows

Poem Comments/ Interpretation

_____
_____
_____
_____
_____
_____
_____
_____
_____
_____
_____
_____
_____
_____
_____
_____
_____
_____
_____
_____
_____
_____
_____
_____
_____
_____
_____

Send Your Comments/*Interpretations* **to Mr. Larry "*Duce*" Cobb**
email address; roxburypoet@yahoo.com

SIX FEET DEEP

Awaken, awaken
From where love doesn't sleep
No return, this one you keep
Love can't be given
Six feet deep
The batter and the battered
Sometimes during the week
A little blood will spatter
Scream, don't scream again
Children hear again and again
Trauma and drama, they wonder
Why can't they just be friends
That's a constant thought
Married or unmarried
Why not, untie the knot
To chase a dream, you've sought
So many before and after
Stayed far, far beyond
Once upon a time, shared laughter
Do you agree, to what came after
Where love has been lost

Death of love, has a cost
Many times it's never found
Hard trying to keep, what's been lost
Where love, understanding and care
Has some how left the building
It's a hellva picture we paint
For the eyes of our children
Is this something
We would like them to repeat.
Answer that
After being battered to sleep
To GOD I pray, you wake up
No return from, six feet deep
Oct 7, 2005

Poem Comments/ Interpretation

_____
_____
_____
_____
_____
_____
_____
_____
_____
_____
_____
_____
_____
_____
_____
_____
_____
_____
_____
_____
_____
_____
_____

Send Your Comments/Interpretations** to Mr. Larry "Duce" Cobb**
email address; roxburypoet@yahoo.com

HAVE YOU BEEN THERE

Every early walking through life
I heard the shaking of the dice
So young thought it was nice
What was heard was some bad advice
What did you hear
Dangerous unknown fear
When for yourself
You had no care
Have you been there
Life started off so right
Eyes caught gleam of city lights
When it was ok to have a fist fight
Hope for tomorrow, died through the night
Once upon a time Lost within a time
Where weakness was no place of mines
Lost control, lost time and mind
Have you been there
Thinking the world owed you everything
To your world, what did you bring
What good went by
While doing the dam thing
Living a sad blues song, by B.B King
Have you been there
Years and years before Michael Jordon
Won his very first slam dunk
Love for self, family, and others
Like the unsinkable Titanic, love sunk
Through the ways, project hallways
Hope came with wishes, of better days
Have you been there

Clouds, wind brought no rain
Death didn't come, it was just pain
This pain I often gave to my Mama
Taking her to the unit trauma
Cause by my drama
Sorry about that Mama
Have you been there
Cooked like a goose, couldn't get loose
Waiting on the gallows being fitted
Just right for the hangman noose
Drugs all around my neck
Had me glad and sad
Always thinking of
The self love I once had
Have you been there
Today I thank GOD for being GOD
He carried me when life
Was cold, bitter and hard
Landing me beyond drugs murk and mire
Putting water on hell's fire
Thank you GOD
For removing that burning desire
Have you been there
Been there, been there
Have you been there
Aug 25 2003

Poem Comments/ Interpretation

Send Your Comments/I*nterpretations to Mr. Larry "Duce" Cobb*

email address; roxburypoet@yahoo.com

SINISTER SCHEME

Sinister scheme
Caught up and lost
Within a bad dream
Deceit has gotten
Ice cold and very mean
It's taken And destroyed the youths
Of Americas dream
Straight from the skillet
To play within the fire
The youth say today
The future is a dam liar
Because gun smoke
Tossing that coke
Rolling that dope
Have them living
At end of the rope
Standing at the tree of life
Hanging with no hope
Broken spirits, lost hope, no faith
Living in quicksand above the waste
No goals, no thoughts of growing old
Blood bath, yellow tape

Any day surrounds a lost soul
See the stories, the front page told
Losing fight with powerful greed
Ghetto sidewalks continue to bleed
Government still down with lowdown deed
Soil of life has taken another seed
The blind are leading the blind
No future in doing more time
Government project, confuses a young mind
Believing to the other, you can't be kind
Hear the spoken word
Who can say, what you heard
Lost within a bad dream
Isn't a sinister scheme
June 28, 2005

Poem Comments/ Interpretation

OPENS THE DOORS

Through my prison bars
For years, and more years
I searched within the stars
Asking GOD, for His mighty help
To remove my soulful scars
Young man, I continue to pray for you
Open your minds, for good to get through
In the days of old, the lost were found
From destruction you can turn it around
With wisdom, knowledge, and understanding
In today's world that's so, so demanding
The guiding light to the stars
Opens the doors, to my prison bars
June 28, 2005

Poem Comments/
Interpretation

_____
_____
_____
_____
_____
_____
_____
_____
_____
_____
_____
_____
_____
_____
_____
_____
_____
_____
_____
_____
_____
_____
_____
_____

WE'VE GOT TO TRUST

Red-rum, red-rum
Pain stuck to hearts
Like hot day, shoes to gum
Wasn't what the church choir
Had to hum
Hopes and prayers
Touches ear that hears
Sounds, of a Mothers tears
Lights went out
On lost hopeful years
Stormy clouds
Not rain but tears
Tears dropped, rain coat
Murder, murder she wrote
Family and friends spoke
Holding back pain, near stroke
Pain doesn't just dissolve
A scream, a scream is heard
What was involved
Police said, not a word
Didn't say may go unsolved
Pain doesn't just dissolve

Can't you and you see
This isn't the way for us to be
Lost love ones, we'll never again see
GOD gave a book, open eyes to see
Helps here for the world, why can't we see
Death to life
Death offers to life
One we can't do twice
Unexpected no show
At the end of life's rainbow
What you thought, you didn't know
Bang, bang, clang, clang
Tears dropped
Church choir sang, and sang
Ashes to ashes, dust to dust
This child memories
Forever belong to us
In GOD
We've got to trust
Sept 3, 2004

Poem Comments/ Interpretation

_____
_____
_____
_____
_____
_____
_____
_____
_____
_____
_____
_____
_____
_____
_____
_____
_____
_____
_____
_____
_____
_____
_____
_____
_____
_____
_____
_____
_____
_____
_____

Send Your Comments/Interpretations to Mr. Larry "Duce" Cobb
email address; roxburypoet@yahoo.com

THAT WILL NEVER INCREASE

Your very own history
To you, it's a mystery
Your life's at risk
Just a broken promise
What did you miss
Time, time for you
It won't, and will not return
Some to many don't live
What you learn, learning
From what you earned
Living that fast shit
Gun shots, gun shots
Are you hit
That's some of what you get
Living that fast shit
A message to a young life
Before you, you see your life
After you leave
Don't follow me please, please
Message reads on and on
Divide yourself
From the weak, to be strong
Young, and younger man
Message of truth, understand
Through your life, have a plan
Planning to fail, you failed to plan
Tomb stone read
Be not like your homies
Live in peace
They left behind memories
That will never increase
Dec 15, 2002

Poem Comments/ Interpretation

_____
_____
_____
_____
_____
_____
_____
_____
_____
_____
_____
_____
_____
_____
_____
_____
_____
_____
_____
_____
_____
_____
_____
_____
_____
_____
_____
_____
_____
_____

Send Your Comments/_Interpretations_ to Mr. Larry "Duce" Cobb
email address; roxburypoet@yahoo.com

HAD TO PLAY

The have not's or have, have
School of many blessing, and lesions
Started at the corner
Of Columbus, and Mass Ave
As all nights, and days
Through silent's you learn
The game, and how to play
To play up on ways to earn
Through a tough ghetto day
Had to play, this way, that's every day
Lots of change, some very strange
Saturday night special, rang out, bang, bang
Gyp joint's band played on
Rhythm, and blues singers sang and sang
Had to play, from that day
To the moments of this day
If you were there, you're with them
What went on around, and in the Big M
Bout the soil of growth of a hoodlum
Wasn't what the church choir had for a hum
Things went down in back room
Seen by outsiders, sudden doom
Some insiders felt the gloom
By what was seen, done in back room
Had to play, young, and in life's prime
Names not known, shared the wine
Some times, not all the time
Neighborhood wine-o great mind
Said whatever you do, be ruthless , sometimes kind
After these lesions, no need to question

Have to count your blessings
To sit in on another session
After playing eat the peg
Left that behind, learned not to beg
Help the table, sit it on full
T-bone stakes, bacon an eggs
Horn the razors edge
Had to play, just that way
From then to now, it's the same
Rules are rules
Play the dam game
Keep it sharp your mind, that's your tool
Then take aim
Had to play
Sept 11, 2003

Poem Comments/ Interpretation

_____
_____
_____
_____
_____
_____
_____
_____
_____
_____
_____
_____
_____
_____
_____
_____
_____
_____
_____
_____
_____
_____
_____
_____
_____

Send Your Comments/Interpretations to Mr. Larry "Duce" Cobb
email address; roxburypoet@yahoo.com

PLACED IN

Memories serve me correct
Through words you hear next
These I protect and respect
The picture I'm about to paint
Shows no sign of a saint
This one, Picasso couldn't paint
Doing this is a pleasure
This love has no measure
Cause it's done
For an absolute treasure
SATIN TOP, SATIN TOP
I hope and Pray,
No one says for me to stop
I want you to hear this up top
It's a step for love
About you, the one we love
Sent to you on the wings of a dove
Fast, fast talker
Fast, fast walker
With a prance,
Under the street lights, through project hallways
Anywhere, everywhere he could tap dance
With a loving romance
SATIN TOP would dance
On the other hand, understand, or misunderstand
Charlie kept a plan
Giving shop keepers not an ounce of relief
Keeping them in disbelief

Their defense was Charlie's offense
Leaving them wondering and wondering
To Charlie that made sense
Just another broken defense
When I think of Charlie
My thoughts are his compliments, with many
smiles
So many showed up for the test
But they had to slide back with the rest
Sorry! Stand up and stomp down
Consistently Charlie dressed the BEST
Whether Winter, Spring, Summer or Fall
My brother, my brother
Suited up for them all
Now that's a memory all of Roxbury can recall
Things I saw him do, stuff I heard he did
Charlie dressed and played the part
With a smile touching a passing heart
This is the kind of stuff
PLACED IN
The Museum of Fine Arts
Oct, 27, 2004

Poem Comments/ Interpretation

Send Your Comments/Interpretations to Mr. Larry "Duce" Cobb
email address; roxburypoet@yahoo.com

DIARY OF A THUG

Straight out of
The diary of a thug
Good, bad, and ugly
Love couldn't get a hug
Peace wouldn't be still
Where it uses to live
Shit roll up and down hill
Any day it can kill
Trouble and more trouble
Day by day, they seem to double
Round here, they'll bust your bubble
Flying high, gun down in May
Happened round the other way
GOD saved a thug that day
Though it went down over there
That's everyday shit around here
Just another thug shown no care
The hood's armed, and up in rage
Dairy, nothing written no this page
Night after, sounds of twelve gage
Within the shadows you stand alone
Love isn't found away from home
Ghetto's streets, you're on your own
Life's short when it's lived wrong
Funeral parlor, church choirs sad song
Streets, like Howard U. or going to Yale
Dreams are made, or on you they set sail
No money for bail, heading straight to jail

Fast, fast learners stay in schools
Yours and My Mama gave us the tools
For fools, schools, and the golden rules
To grow out of empty lots, and broken glass
Understand, these lesions very well
Because Daddy said, it's your black ass
It's a thugs test all want to pass
Mama's baby boy
Left alone his play toy
For a life, he would destroy
It didn't cross the mind's eye
Knowing nothing, bout live or die
That one I can't deny
Nickels, dimes, quarters, and dollar
That shit, will make you pop your collar
Top of the world Mama, you'll holler, holler
Famous words, of a once upon time baller
Daddy here, Mama's gone wish I could call-her
To quiche a thirst,
I run with the worst
Wandering between life and death,
Which comes first
Searching for the best
A hood's ghetto test
Praying, hoping, and wishing
You don't fall, six feet to rest
Time no return, lesions you learn
Heaven, or hell which ever you'll earn
Sender or receiver of that letter

We call it a kite from up state
Wait till freedom has a date
What do you do, after long, long wait
Living within the eye
Of complete danger
This Mother's child
Isn't some kind of stranger
Moment by moment, change without change
Life's in danger
Good, bad and ugly
Love couldn't get a hug
Straight out of
Dairy of a thug
Nov 16, 2004

Poem Comments/ Interpretation

IT CAN HAPPEN

This is about a journey
That began seven years ago
Back then I had no idea
How the rivers of life would flow
What I did need was God
To show me which way to go
Before that Satan had me
Since then God has set me free
It can happen to you
Everybody knows it happened to me
Trials and tribulations
Countless temptations
Has been near and far
Since being baptized in the congregation
August 8, 2007

Poem Comments/ Interpretation

WHAT'S LOST

Why you want
To build a rep off me
When our Ancestors
Traveled oceans and deep blue seas
In chains being taken places
They had no desire, to ever be
Divisions is, the greatest divide
What's not so funny, the truth they hide
Portraying us bader than bad
Even after stealing, the joy we once had
As I be writing this, I think
Of my Ancestors, the hood where lives sink
Many giving all they had left
Gunshots, the hood another death
Beyond this, what else will be taken
God commands have been forsaken
Peace shattered, Love broken
What's lost here aint no MBTA token
April 1, 2004

Poem Comments/ Interpretation

_____
_____
_____
_____
_____
_____
_____
_____
_____
_____
_____
_____
_____
_____
_____
_____
_____
_____
_____
_____
_____
_____
_____
_____
_____

Send Your Comments/Interpretations to Mr. Larry "Duce" Cobb
email address; roxburypoet@yahoo.com

DROP THE TEAR

Through the days
Of our lives
We get touched and stung
Chasing honey at a bee's hive
Hotter than hot
Meltdown isn't sought
Did you hear
Some have it, some not
Either you rise
Or you are sure to fall
By your own bad advise
Broken dreams
Lying to yourself
Because of you
You blame everyone else
No need to sit around
Living today's life in sorrow
Guess what, the same will come
In search for tomorrow
What's it going to be
Be to going to what
It's a rollercoaster ride
From yourself, you can't hide
Echo's old folks said
Young people use your head
Be careful how you make your bed
Because you'll lie in it
Alive or dead
Did you hear
It's hard living one year
To play the game of life
Without care
Drop, drop the tear..............................
March 12, 2003

Poem Comments/ Interpretation

THE ACTIONS, TODAY

If he was here today,
About the 21st century
Just ah going astray
Where the lost, lost their way
What on earth would Jesus say
Seeing all written, in the good book
Taken for granted, like food mama would cook
No understanding, we lost the book
Blinded by wine, coke, and dope
Now we sleep with the fish, bait on the hook
Look all around, take a good look
What on earth, would Jesus say
Seeing the world, going over the edge
Where wrong and wrong, make a pledge
To leave behind, God given knowledge
Watching the news, the stories tell
Souls are told, why not out right sell
Wisdom, knowledge, and understanding
Doesn't live in a dried up well
The actions, today say welcome to Hell
If he was here today
About the 21st century
Just ah going astray
Where the lost, lost their way
What on earth would Jesus say
Toady
Today
Today
The actions today
May 13, 2006

Poem Comments/ Interpretation

IT'S HEARD

Across the Red Sea
Through wilderness
To the promise land,
We can get there
When we understand
What my mother would say
She could see through
Muddy waters, and see dry land
To stand on, in the face of fear
Go forward, you can get there
Life's a heavy bout
Leave behind any doubt
There's nothing wrong
With trying it out
Freedom isn't bondage
Break the mental chains
Of being a self made hostage
Then stamp, and address the chains
With a no return postage
Growth doesn't happen on it's own
Living life isn't done all alone
Families, friends, and strangers have shown
When it is, many go over the edge
Why do we have to lose another one
Who got lost with lost knowledge
Speaking for myself I make this pledge
To take a better look at the picture
Searching for the missing treasure
Those things that bring God pleasure
Truth, nothing about life is hard
Knowledge, Wisdom, and Understanding
It's heard, the words of God...........
Oct 5, 2005

Poem Comments/
Interpretation

THE REASON FOR THE CALL

There's a biblical call
Not for one, but for all
Who understands some of the
Reasons for the call
Where we've gone far away
Actions say, we've gone astray
By the things going on
Yesterday and now today
Back in time, it was a rain flood
Streets now, covered with young blood
Stain after stain mixed with mud
Rain of homicide has risen to a flood
Fear adds to the measure
Good has become a lost treasure
As I write this piece
I wander to a time, when life was a pleasure
The glass of life's half full
When you don't know, who you're riding with
The power of Satan it's like a raging bull
On the weak and the strong he continues to pull
There's a biblical call
Not for one, but for all
Who understands some of the reasons for the
call...........................

Aug 10, 2006

Poem Comments/ Interpretation

WHAT HAPPENED

Where has kindness gone
That stuff written, and said
Through an everyday love song
How did things go so wrong
Because the low down blues
Has taken the center stage
Playing on stress and outrage
Haven't you read the stories
That cover the whole front page
What happened to God's rules
For the wise and the damn fools
Believe it, truth's delivered this way
Music plays by it's own rules
Today they continue to play and play
Day after day those low down blues
What happened, to God's rules
June 19, 2005

Poem Comments/ Interpretation

GOD MAY ONLY KNOW

Over my shoulder
There's no need to look
Because I gave up
Living my life, as a crook
Don't even bother, to ask
Can't always play, by the good book
I'm not what I want to be
I'm not what I use to be
Who I am, the whole world can see
I've journeyed through the mountains
Traveled within the alleys, and valleys
That place where the good
And the ugly bad angel fell
I've seen Heaven, made visits to Hell
Always thanking God
For the story I now tell
So as above, so as below
I'm just dropping this so you know
So much has gone down the river
What happens from here
God may only know.........................
May 3, 2006

Poem Comments/
Interpretation

CHAOS

Living in a world
Surrounded by chaos
Love, hope and faith
Has a way of getting lost
Temptation stands on call
Saying it's ok, it's ok
To turn back on God
Chaos says I'll break the fall
The price of chaos
Many can not afford
The price is to damn high
Who wants to take a loss
Watching good go to bad
This aint a TV movie
That you watched or had
This picture's painted sad
Showing young and old
Forsaking life long goals
Then Satan takes hold
Leading them to other lost souls
Here, goods hard to find
Some hope and hope for the better
Evil has never ever sent
Anybody a Dear John letter
March 7, 2008

Poem Comments/ Interpretation

_____

_____

_____

_____

_____

_____

_____

_____

_____

_____

_____

_____

_____

_____

_____

_____

_____

_____

_____

_____

_____

_____

_____

_____

_____

_____

_____

_____

Send Your Comments/Interpretations to Mr. Larry "Duce" Cobb
email address; roxburypoet@yahoo.com

SILENCE

My silence is golden
That's always been my goal
A keeper of many stories
Not to ever be told
Bout the playing of the game
I've been taught, it's sold not told
This aint just about me
It's deeper than an ocean
Rougher than a stormy sea
I had to go through it
I'm not untouchable, but don't touch me
Been on the front line
Where others lost their mind
Lived with the changing of time
I Thank God, I've got my mind
Oct 19, 2007

Poem Comments/ Interpretation

MAMA AND BABY GIRL

All around me
They sit, work, talk and stand
When I look at them, I see me
If not for women, I wouldn't be
To men and the universe
The ladies are the world
Through them we've come
Thank God for grand ma,   .
Mama and baby girl
April 26, 2007

Poem Comments/ Interpretation

ON YOUR OWN

Being chased
Fear is it's name
Avoiding face to face
Between there's no space
So many run
Like shade from the sun
Where hope seems done
God knows this aint fun
Some learn to bob
Others practice the weave
Ali floated like a butterfly
Fears sting aint no lie
In a crowd or alone
Behind doors, on your own
Dec 2, 2007

Poem Comments/ Interpretation

WHICH WAS LEFT

Some places I've been
Standing all alone
Other times with my best friend
Walking and running thick and thin
Some have, others haven't
Been through shadow of death
Through the Grace of God
Didn't give life which was left
Jan 14, 2008

Poem Comments/ Interpretation

_____
_____
_____
_____
_____
_____
_____
_____
_____
_____
_____
_____
_____
_____
_____
_____
_____
_____
_____
_____
_____
_____
_____
_____
_____
_____
_____

Send Your Comments/Interpretations to Mr. Larry "Duce" Cobb
email address; roxburypoet@yahoo.com

WE JUST DON'T KNOW

Have you ever been
Where beauty came to live
Their strangers, became friends
Loneliness left behind
To move with more to give
Strangers came to be friends
Beauty itself came alive to live
This place many have never been
Round and round we go
Where good stops
We just don't know
Jan 6, 2008

Poem Comments/ Interpretation

_____
_____
_____
_____
_____
_____
_____
_____
_____
_____
_____
_____
_____
_____
_____
_____
_____
_____
_____
_____
_____
_____
_____
_____
_____
_____
_____
_____
_____

Send Your Comments/_Interpretations to Mr. Larry "Duce" Cobb_
email address; roxburypoet@yahoo.com

TRUTH WAS GIVEN

From young to old
Before and after
Good , bad or sad
What happened to the laughter
Remember the sound
As mama's baby and Gods child
Into life not knowing it was laughter
This sound may not
Open doors to Heaven
But it sho-nuff will
Close the doors to Hell
Haven't you heard
Or read the Bible, stories they tell
Truth was given through spoken word
Jan 16, 2005

Poem Comments/ Interpretation

WHERE'S THE TRUST

If you want
The best out of me
You've got to give
The best out of you
To climb the mountains
Walk beyond the valleys
That we're sure to go through
The very best come from me, you
Care lives with love and pain
It doesn't disappear in the rain
It's the water of growing pain
That makes what's to be maintain
No need to get up a fuss
The rules don't change for us
To keep what we got is a must
When I'm here and you're there
Help me! Where's the trust

Sept 1, 2007

Poem Comments/ Interpretation

_____
_____
_____
_____
_____
_____
_____
_____
_____
_____
_____
_____
_____
_____
_____
_____
_____
_____
_____
_____
_____
_____
_____
_____
_____
_____

ANTICIPATION

The distance is far
But there's no stopping
Waiting for me
To get from where you are
I'm home all alone
Times passing by slow
Hoping it rings, the phone
Here together we're not alone
The door opens
Up stairs we go
Another door opens
Just inside there we go
With our clothes on
Now clothes are gone
Hands going everywhere
Anticipation grown strong
Sept 17, 2007

Poem Comments/ Interpretation

_____
_____
_____
_____
_____
_____
_____
_____
_____
_____
_____
_____
_____
_____
_____
_____
_____
_____
_____
_____
_____
_____
_____
_____
_____
_____
_____
_____

Send Your Comments/Interpretations to Mr. Larry "Duce" Cobb
email address; roxburypoet@yahoo.com

FAREWELL

First I thank God
For allowing Jalanie Nicole John
To come by our way
Only to touch us with her very best
Heavens no longer missing an Angel
Now she's gone back home
Leaving us with memories of our own
Whether they be happy or sad
To me she was my sister
With sister I already had
Time seems to, to short
Forever I'll be so glad
For the memories we had
Writing this I've shed a tear
Because you're not here
Thank you for being family
Years and years after another year
Only God, Family and loved ones
Knows you will be missed down here
May God Bless you,
Rest In Peace, FAREWELL
Nov 26, 2007

Poem Comments/
Interpretation

WHAT GOD HAS DONE

Once you become removed
Above living on the ground
To others nothing to be proved
Growth has it's own sound
Stop, look and listen
Pitfall ahead, pay attention
Mama said, child go slow
She wouldn't speak
What she didn't know
Mentally and physically stay able
Spiritually keep it on the table
Feast on stories the Bible told
God saved the wandering soul
On dangerous roads we've paved
From death and destruction, I was saved
Out of one hundred
I was the lost one
Today I'm thankful for
What God has done..........................
July 29, 2001

Poem Comments/ Interpretation

NEVER EVER STOPS

Away from God
The x'd out Angel fell
Believe you can break
That unforgiving spell
Knowledge of God
Is the road out of Hell
At the crossroads of life
Between the old and the new
Going nowhere, aint nothing new
What God did for me
I do believe, God can do for you
Once lost now found
Victory for yourself
Rise from the ground
Living with surround sound
After school of hard knocks
Game of life never ever stops
Jan 7, 2008

Poem Comments/
Interpretation

_____
_____
_____
_____
_____
_____
_____
_____
_____
_____
_____
_____
_____
_____
_____
_____
_____
_____
_____
_____
_____
_____
_____
_____
_____
_____
_____
_____
_____
_____

Send Your Comments/_Interpretations to Mr. Larry "Duce" Cobb_
email address; roxburypoet@yahoo.com

HE LOVE'S TO DO

Kicked from Beyond the sun
Landing on earth
The thief of souls
Of daughters and a son
He's the wrong, to right
The one who lost the fight
His darkness couldn't stand
The almighty, God's light
God is, the giver of good
If you don't know you should
It's taught at Church in the hood
Mama hopes, wishes, and prays
You and all your homies give up
The bad and ugly, for plenty good
The cruel one's the taker
A world famous faker
Leading souls to the undertaker
A relative's heart breaker
God's the giver, by all means
He's not the taker, he's your maker
Just look at what he's done for you
Remember, remember, remember
Troubles, problems you lived through
People can say what they want
The cruel one
Thief of souls
God's love is true
Sharing his love,
He loves to do
Sept 5, 2003

Poem Comments/ Interpretation

GIVEN BY GOD

Running late to work
By bus, train, to a train
Things meeting me on time
Being late wasn't on my mind
My last train arrives
It's empty, I enter to sit
Backward seat, going forward
People intertwine their lives
With much good reason
The all seeing eye sees
Where others are blind
Good has come in season
Empty seat beside me
It's taken by one who can see
My blackness is me
Given by God, for the world to see...................
Dec 27, 2007

Poem Comments/
Interpretation

_____
_____
_____
_____
_____
_____
_____
_____
_____
_____
_____
_____
_____
_____
_____
_____
_____
_____
_____
_____
_____
_____

Send Your Comments/Interpretations to Mr. Larry "Duce" Cobb
email address; roxburypoet@yahoo.com

TO THIS TODAY

On this, the sun rose
A blessing came to be
Eyes opened, only to see
What God has done for me
On this, the sun rose
Awake first breath of air
Given to meet me right there
To inhale God's loving care
On this, the sun rose
Greeted with will, to be strong
What God has done, I do belong
On this, the sun rose
Feb 4, 2007

Poem Comments/ Interpretation

_____

_____

_____

_____

_____

_____

_____

_____

_____

_____

_____

_____

_____

_____

_____

_____

_____

_____

_____

_____

_____

_____

_____

NOW I'M FOUND

I'm talking about
A desert, through a drought
Surviving beyond all doubt
I made it out, hope you make it out
So many were left behind
Looking forward, they come to mind
How we treated our lives so unkind
Not to mention doing that State time
It's hard running
Chasing a hearse
Just to be first
On all that I love
I rolled with the worst
Like a thirsty man
Just to quench a thirst
Others left in a hearse
As I, you'll pay the cost
That's said, cause once I was lost
Gambling with my life
Didn't hear, old folks advice
Living that life, aint nice
Believe it or not, there's only one life
I didn't hear one sound
Now I thank God for being God
I'm not six feet underground
Through God's Mercy and Grace
Once I was lost, now I'm found
Oct 26, 2005

Poem Comments/ Interpretation

_____
_____
_____
_____
_____
_____
_____
_____
_____
_____
_____
_____
_____
_____
_____
_____
_____
_____
_____
_____
_____
_____
_____
_____
_____
_____
_____
_____
_____

Send Your Comments/_Interpretations_ to Mr. Larry "Duce" Cobb
email address; roxburypoet@yahoo.com

WE'VE LIVED WITHIN

Given on the wings
Of a dove,
Only GOD could've
Granted us this
From Heaven above
That thing, that thing called love
Together we've come to touch
Not all, but some of a bunch
Of things others hope, wish
And pray for so very much
Afterwards came the wake
This others and some can't take
Death of love, is a mistake
Birth of a sad blues song
Question, where on earth
Did we go so very wrong
There I am, again and again
Nowhere to go, home alone
Trying not to look and wait
For her call to ring my phone
Loneliness is working on me
Cause her face constantly I see
Across the room stands her picture
Within my heart she's a treasure
My my my, she helped life, to be a pleasure
I hear the cries, I hear the cries
The same as my heart now cries
Of the caged bird who couldn't sing
If I said I didn't want for us
To have the very best of all things
GOD knows that's a pack of lies
Do you hear the cries, the cries
Of the caged bird who wouldn't sing
That's life, that's life

That thing where love was taken
From where it would once sing
Two rights, can straighten any wrong
Whether with me, or long gone
Our precious moments
We've lived within, a love song.....
Sept 3, 2005

Poem Comments/ Interpretation

_____
_____
_____
_____
_____
_____
_____
_____
_____
_____
_____
_____
_____
_____
_____
_____
_____
_____
_____
_____
_____
_____
_____
_____
_____
_____
_____
_____
_____
_____

Send Your Comments/Interpretations to Mr. Larry "Duce" Cobb
email address; roxburypoet@yahoo.com

WHAT'S TO END

Everyone searches
For a rainbow with
A pot of gold at the end
Others want to find
The four leaf clover
To be lucky at the end
I'm deeply in the hunt
For a genie in the bottle
So I'll be able to climb in
With all good intention
To climb high above a lover
Where eagles soar, within a friend
Standing very, very still
In the eyes of another storm
So calm touches us in the end
I can see it all now
All of the ways that we start
Keeping that way, what's to end
July 14, 1993

Poem Comments/
Interpretation

_____
_____
_____
_____
_____
_____
_____
_____
_____
_____
_____
_____
_____
_____
_____
_____
_____
_____
_____
_____
_____
_____
_____
_____
_____

Send Your Comments/Interpretations to Mr. Larry "Duce" Cobb
email address; roxburypoet@yahoo.com

CHASE THE SMOKE

Standing at the corner
The house is all white
Inside it's heard,
Someone wanting a light
Fire, fire to burn the rock
To chase the smoke
By inhaling that cloud
That's known as coke
Chase, chase, chase
The young, and the old
Good lives, come to waste
They go to hearing other things
Froze, froze right, right there
In a state of lose being
Chase, chase, chase
On a voyage to
To a far away zone
The house is full
But they're all alone
Now they are up
Still, still beaming
Back to earth, tough luck
Broke, empty they go scheming, scheming

Where's it coming from
Heart racing, beating like a drum
Chase the smoke
It's heard, can I have a piece, that jum
Mind running wild, how to come up
Mind running wild, how to come up
Just one more hit, of that shit
Some do damn near anything
Just to get it
Smoke the chase, chase the smoke
For it, doing it, some driven to a stroke
Now ears begin to ring, ring
Mothers, fathers, sons, baby girl
Holler, holler, want to give it a whirl
Running, running like a marathon race
Hoping money's in pocket, of person they meet
Chase the smoke, smoke the chase
So my man said, he wants a round the world
She says $50, he says for that
I can get 5 girls
No not out his car is she willing to get
Not without getting $10 to suck his dick
Chase the smoke, Smoke the chase
Jan 16, 1995

Poem Comments/
Interpretation

_____
_____
_____
_____
_____
_____
_____
_____
_____
_____
_____
_____
_____
_____
_____
_____
_____
_____
_____
_____
_____
_____
_____
_____
_____
_____

Send Your Comments/_Interpretations_ **to Mr. Larry "Duce" Cobb**
email address; roxburypoet@yahoo.com

THERE'S HOPE

To finding what's to come
Aint the end, it's the beginning
Within the pain to what's been done
Behind the rain stands the sun
Whirlwinds will come, then gone
Making it uncomfortable to be strong
Life's about the right and the wrong
Joy and many tears, fill a blues song
Before the end of the road have a plan
Aint cool living out of a trash can
Where others have fallen, stand
There's hope, when this you understand
March 2, 200

Poem Comments/
Interpretation

_____
_____
_____
_____
_____
_____
_____
_____
_____
_____
_____
_____
_____
_____
_____
_____
_____
_____
_____
_____
_____
_____
_____
_____
_____
_____
_____
_____

Send Your Comments/Interpretations to Mr. Larry "Duce" Cobb
email address; roxburypoet@yahoo.com

WHY CAN'T WE REACH

Why can't we reach
Martins' dream for us
Knock, ask, and seek
God knows he would preach
Peace, Love, Unity and Harmony
That's a tough quilt for us to make
We can do, we have to
It's a must do, to over come
The things that have been done
In the shadows, of the rising sun
For God sake
Our children's children will witness
The reality of Martins' dream
Never-ever was it a mistake
From then to right now
There's more at stake
By the hour, the minute, the seconds
Our very young souls.
Are lost to us daily
Spreading like gangrene
It has gotten much worst
While Satan continues
To quench a bloody thirst
There goes another hearse
This picture it's seen by the day
God knows, this aint the way
To the future of a brighter day
Good is a one way street

That holds the thrill of victory
Not doing anything
We drown in the agony of defeat
For self, family and strangers
Move away from that idle seat
Let the voice of truth be heard
Without a lot of change, what's there to borrow
I'm speaking about, the future of our tomorrow
Here we are surrounded by today's days of sorrow
We must better today, for better tomorrow
We have miles and miles to go.
God and Martin said
For self, family and strangers
Forward we must go
The time says, aint no time to sleep
When it's the dream we pray to keep
Though we've come so very far
From where Martin's dream stood
Love for the other, it's over par
Why can't we reach
The dream of our shining star
Dec 10, 2006

Poem Comments/
Interpretation

_____
_____
_____
_____
_____
_____
_____
_____
_____
_____
_____
_____
_____
_____
_____
_____
_____
_____
_____
_____
_____
_____
_____
_____
_____
_____
_____
_____

OUR FUTURE COURSE

Message to all
North, East, South and West
Can you hear, can you hear
Which one, who can say
This one you haven't heard
Actions speaks louder than words
From all directions, we come
To this God given spot
Here to get something done
God knows being together
We will shine as the sun
Actions today means rearrange
Our thinking and our thoughts
For some it's strange
To hear time, asking for change
To obtain goals we've sought
Share the reward, share the reward
By casting in your lot
Together, we can get
How else can we get
Together, together
Rainbow people,
What we've come so far to get
From ourselves and all others
Under the rainbow of colors

Chase and follow the dream
Touch a star, live a wish
The cries of this call
Living, working through prayer
We're the gift to God's promise
To the races of the people
So as above, so as below
That live under the rainbow
Love, Wisdom, Knowledge and Understanding
Can change the course of how
The river to the future shall flow
Did you hear action speaking
The minister, the preacher preaching
Did you hear mama in the kitchen
Cooking, talking, all the time teaching
My, my, my that's action speaking
With a touch of love
Respect and care
From here to there
We are the source
To changing the tide
Our future course
April 4, 2005

Poem Comments/
Interpretation

_____
_____
_____
_____
_____
_____
_____
_____
_____
_____
_____
_____
_____
_____
_____
_____
_____
_____
_____
_____
_____
_____
_____
_____
_____

Send Your Comments/*Interpretations* to Mr. Larry "Duce" Cobb
email address; roxburypoet@yahoo.com

MEMORIES

As summer came back
So did I, to memories
Of a more joyful time
Could it be due
To the weather
Or was it a time
That was much better
So as it comes
It goes the season
The bench I sit on
Now gives good reason
Why I've come here today
Thoughts of the lady
Just won't go away
The bad is gone
The memories are here to stay
Memories
Of a loving yesterday..........
July 2, 2005

Poem Comments/ Interpretation

JUST TALKING BOUT

It's not about preaching
This all came about
Through life's many teachings
Where some came to stop
At places others kept reaching
For one of the goals
They've always been seeking
There's no better time
To tap within the mind
So to see as a child
To live in the now of the time
As it's always been said
Life is, prime time
The game of life
You can't win today
With yesterdays home run
Just talkin bout
Getting something done
Every day of precious life
Is a wonder to see
What God has done.........................
Sept 16, 2005

Poem Comments/
Interpretation

Send Your Comments/Interpretations to Mr. Larry "Duce" Cobb
email address; roxburypoet@yahoo.com

TAKE THE RIGHT TURN

No, I'm not the first nor last
To live a thought
Of touching a dream
Overcoming the obstacles
That come and go as I pass
These thoughts came
When I was young and fast
Where death and destruction
Was the meal at the feast
Some didn't make it out the playground
Where we played, in the belly of the beast
It's hard for some to believe
God saved and blessed me
To turn over a new leaf
As I others can do it too
Realizing in the mind, house is surrounded
You can run and hide, but not from you
Lost time, lost mind, one can return
Standing at the crossroads of life
What do you do, with lessons you learn
Heaven's a blessing, hell you burn
Caution sign, stop, look and listen
Take the right turn...........................
July 30, 2005

Poem Comments/ Interpretation

STANDING IN THE RAIN

Standing in the rain
Being washed clean, by God
After being lifted up
From going down the drain
Rev. Baker Bey, stood with me
Tears blurred sight, couldn't see
The miracle given to me
Looking back
There's nothing to see
Above sure death, destruction
Years and years of drug addiction
God gave me a blessing to live
That love only God can give
From going down the drain
After being lifted up
Being washed clean, by God
Standing in the rain
Dec 4, 2007

Poem Comments/ Interpretation

_____
_____
_____
_____
_____
_____
_____
_____
_____
_____
_____
_____
_____
_____
_____
_____
_____
_____
_____
_____
_____
_____
_____
_____
_____

Send Your Comments/Interpretations to Mr. Larry "Duce" Cobb
email address; roxburypoet@yahoo.com

OUT OF TOUCH

Beyond the womb
Before the tomb
Open the door to
God's precious room
There it's found, promise
When two or more pray
Answers come like this
This boat, please don't miss
Otherwise, down the river
Floating with nowhere to go
Water won't stop the fire
That Hell will blow
These are the days of our lives
That offers so, so much
Ask yourself, what's the feeling
Of being out of touch....................
Dec 21,2007

Poem Comments/
Interpretation

_____
_____
_____
_____
_____
_____
_____
_____
_____
_____
_____
_____
_____
_____
_____
_____
_____
_____
_____
_____
_____
_____
_____
_____
_____

Send Your Comments/Interpretations to Mr. Larry "Duce" Cobb
email address; roxburypoet@yahoo.com

JOY AND PAIN

Within the lonely
Hollows of my mind
Thoughts of you
Spend their time
So many memories
Never to go away
Lived endless love stories
Since meeting that day
There we were
You and I
Destiny for us
We couldn't deny
The future of destiny
There's no divide
Joy and pain
Come with the ride.............................
Oct 5, 2002

Poem Comments/ Interpretation

ONLY TO STAY

Talking bout love
That comes and goes
Where it stops, to stay
Nobody knows, nobody knows
That's loves mystery
The love of love
Writes it's own history
Intertwined by it
Sorry! It's still a mystery
Searching and searching for it
It's like looking for a gold mine
Hopefully it touches you
Only to stay, a life time..............................
Jan 1, 2007

Poem Comments/
Interpretation

TOUCH THE STARS

It's about
Keeping our love
Together in areas
Where others fail
On the journey
Where love of love
Shall take us
We can't forget
What it's built on
Trust and more trust
While we accept
One another as they are
Then and only then
Will we be able to
Touch the stars........................
May 6, 2001

Poem Comments/ Interpretation

Send Your Comments/Interpretations to Mr. Larry "Duce" Cobb
email address; roxburypoet@yahoo.com

NOTHING TO FIND

In the valley
Of the lost soul
There's a no show
Cause hope was stopped
Before it reached, it's goal
Trying to reach wisdom
Who lives with knowledge
And a friend, understanding
In a world that's so demanding
Mind living in war zone
It's hard being left alone
Between unseen and unknown
Trouble can't live alone
It's not a good time
Seeing young wasted minds
Searching for nothing
There's nothing to find...................................
Oct 18, 2006

Poem Comments/ Interpretation

_____

_____

_____

_____

_____

_____

_____

_____

_____

_____

_____

_____

_____

_____

_____

_____

_____

_____

_____

_____

_____

_____

_____

_____

_____

_____

_____

Send Your Comments/Interpretations to Mr. Larry "Duce" Cobb
email address; roxburypoet@yahoo.com

BEYOND

*Sometimes I be speakin
Bout things I'm thinkin
Some may think I'm preachin
Little do they know, it's teachin
Bout there's a way out
Beyond fear and doubt
Date unknown*

Poem Comments/ Interpretation

_____
_____
_____
_____
_____
_____
_____
_____
_____
_____
_____
_____
_____
_____
_____
_____
_____
_____
_____
_____
_____
_____
_____
_____
_____
_____

Send Your Comments/Interpretations to Mr. Larry "Duce" Cobb
email address; roxburypoet@yahoo.com

WHY SHOULD THIS END

Even after our love
Flew so high, then it fell
Still, I wish you well
In my heart of hearts
Who can replace, the likes of you
Beyond the places, we've been to
We've crossed a rainbow
Shared a pot, of that inside gold
Where we bared to the other, the soul
While there both looked within
To see the mirror, of a friend
Losers can't win, why should this
end..............................
May 21, 2006

Poem Comments/
Interpretation

WAS PLEASED

Since you came
Into my life
My days and nights
Aint the same
Heaven is where
You use to live
Becoming the gift to me
Only God can give
Sending you to earth
Like the autumn leaves
Floating on a cool breeze
I've come to believe
With the making of you
God himself, was pleased....................
Feb 14, 2004

Poem Comments/ Interpretation

IT CAN'T BE WRONG

In my way of thinking
You're all I'll ever need
To forever brighten my day
I'm more than thankful
We met along the way
In my journey through life
I've thought of, the likes of you
Never-ever expecting
To find the likes of you
My, my, my, was I so, so wrong
Some days it's unbelievable
Living our own love song
Keeping a love like this
It can't be wrong...........................
Feb 2, 2001

Poem Comments/ Interpretation

THE SAME AS I DO

May the wings
Of every Angel
Keep the reason to
Surround your bed
To heal you
To protect you
To love you
The same as I do
Nov 1, 2006

Poem Comments/ Interpretation

PLEASE, PLEASE GO HOME

On the rise, and rising
Only to fall summer of 1968
The days of hope, was told
Hold up, it had to wait
Seconds of feeling pressure
Confusion stole the concert
Understanding had no date
Heart felt pain with no escape
The spark of sparks was lit
Although young, I was in it
What happened didn't seem to fit
Cities burned and burned
Just because of it
One shot with surround sound
Word came, hearts dropped to the ground
Shock strangled Boston's Beantown
Down Mass Ave, walked James Brown
Saying Please, Please go home
My memories see him walking and talking
Without a bodyguard in sight
Saying Please, Please go home
Sept 19, 2007

Poem Comments/ Interpretation

MAKE A SOUND

On the way to work
Beyond the bus windows
It was seen, pain and hurt
Sad is, what I see
Is an awful fact
Once upon a time
That there was me
Early morning
Walking the street
Life in agony of defeat
Care for self gone
Living a sad blues song
Walking lost
Going nowhere
Spirit broken and torn apart
Seeing this picture
Touches my heart
In a maze
Praying for better days
Look up, not just down
God hears help, help
When you make a sound
May 24, 2002

Poem Comments/ Interpretation

THE GAME HAS A COST

Life's a main event show
Through Hell and high water
You got to live it, to know
All don't get a pass to go
Many are left far behind
Cause some got caught in a bind
Can't step away, doing State time
There freedom, stays on the mind
What I write, I've been there
This story I had to share
To hear the truth it's rare
I share it with the youths
Cause I care, avoid this despair
If at your age I only knew
This I would have to go through
God knows, I'd found better to do
With the life I had to live through
Never thought I'd love any letter
Even if it was one of those, Dear John
You know I will always love you,
But baby I'm moving on, I've found better
Or like me, my mother I lost
That some of what happens
Once upon a time, you was the boss
Your spot it's taken, the game has a cost
In this game, much is found and all is lost
Sept 1, 2006

Poem Comments/
Interpretation

_____
_____
_____
_____
_____
_____
_____
_____
_____
_____
_____
_____
_____
_____
_____
_____
_____
_____
_____
_____
_____
_____

Send Your Comments/Interpretations to Mr. Larry "Duce" Cobb
email address; roxburypoet@yahoo.com

I ROSE, I ROSE

I rose, I rose
Beyond Satan, buying my soul
In the middle of my search for gold
Never thinking, from myself, I stole
I rose, I rose
Been through the furnace
Again, again and again
Didn't care how life would end
God himself, pulled me out again
I rose, I rose
Above wine, coke and dope
Down there belief said, without it
There wouldn't be a way to cope
Outside the belly of the beast
It's tough, living beyond no hope
I rose, I rose
To where I now stand
Mama said, it's more to be a man
She's gone I hear, do you understand
Now that you've risen, above the quicksand
The hand to hold you, is God's plan
I rose, I rose
July 16, 2006

Poem Comments/
Interpretation

_____
_____
_____
_____
_____
_____
_____
_____
_____
_____
_____
_____
_____
_____
_____
_____
_____
_____
_____
_____
_____
_____
_____
_____
_____
_____
_____

Send Your Comments/Interpretations to Mr. Larry "Duce" Cobb
email address; roxburypoet@yahoo.com

WHAT OTHERS SEEK

So, so many seek
With much, much hope
And a wish to find
What we secretly keep
Within our hearts, and minds
Through reality
Our good has come
About our joy, and fun
Reaching heights never done
Understanding to understand
In a world of great demand
It happened without a plan
Care for the other
It was put in place to withstand
Sharing soulful laughter
We've grown, and grown to touch
Some of what we're after
Laughter after laughter
Our stillness runs very deep
It's awake, it's awake
Never ever does it sleep
What we have, and hold
It's for us to keep
That thing, that thing
What others seek.....................
Date unknown

Poem Comments/ Interpretation

THAT'S A PICTURE

History of stories
There's much to say
Bout it today and yesterday
Stories of histories
Life's full of mysteries
Seen where they are seen
Within family or a stranger
In plain view or rear view
Schemes falling short of a dream
The world goes cold, cold mean
Joke it aint, some say revoke
Here, there it's everywhere
Coke continues to go up in smoke
The meltdown of this reaches many
Victimized beyond a stroke
Lineup that started, now decline
Some stop saying, life's been on the line
Still families and strangers stand in line
Wine drowns others, Willy wine-o great mind
That's a picture, which will never be kind
Feb 2, 2007

Poem Comments/ Interpretation

LIFE WITH ANOTHER

Sugar, stand with me
Back to back, left and right
So together, we'll journey
From darkness into the light
Let's be there for the other
When we're up, surely when down
Whether we are talking
Or just there without a sound
Life with another
Has many twists, and many turns
From the climb of mountains
To down below the valleys
There's lessons for us to learn
Life without another
Never should we touch
Feelings of being alone
Cause we're the caretakers
To all the love we own
Life with another
Affection and more affection
One having it for the other
Has a way of keeping both strong
The journey won't be short, but long......................
June 29, 2001

Poem Comments/ Interpretation

GET SOMETHING DONE

My, my, my
What a sight
The rising sun
Chance to live
Again has come
Pray, love, work
Have some fun
Before night falls
Get something done........................
Jan 1, 2007

Poem Comments/ Interpretation

Send Your Comments/Interpretations to Mr. Larry "Duce" Cobb
email address; roxburypoet@yahoo.com

FILLED WITH OUR DEAD

The commander and chief
Keeps world in disbelief
Who said he's not a thief
Under his reign, no relief
For no good, he robbed and stole
Power with no thought, it's bold
Taking oil, turning it into gold
Atop of young and younger dying souls
Making the world so, so afraid
Quite a mess he himself has made
The people wonder will it fade
Silently, and aloud families prayed
Price of living raised by the boss
What else after lives will it cost
Empire before us fell from within
Bad leadership, we stand at a lost
God knows where we're doomed to head
Cause he keeps on putting us in a hot bed
With no help for the people, or what's said
Speaking about graveyards, filled with our
dead....................
Jan 24, 2004

Poem Comments/ Interpretation

_____
_____
_____
_____
_____
_____
_____
_____
_____
_____
_____
_____
_____
_____
_____
_____
_____
_____
_____
_____
_____
_____
_____
_____
_____
_____
_____
_____
_____

Send Your Comments/Interpretations to Mr. Larry "Duce" Cobb
email address; roxburypoet@yahoo.com

REASON I'M HERE TODAY

Within the many years
Of heartache and tears
God carried me
All of those many years
As I ran and lived through
The valley of the shadow of death
God stopped Lucifer from taking
The only life I had left
As a desert, hopes for rain
Hope for me was, God removed the pain
Cause the life I lived was insane
Rain I prayed for, to cover the pain
To wash away the years of tear drop stains
Even back then I would pray
I worked for no one, looking for pay
Surprise, secure and the getaway
Pray I did, cause I lived that way
Beyond what I knew to be cold and mean
These eyes and heart of mine have seen
The Gospel truth, on God you can lean
After lies and more than one scheme
My world didn't crumble, after broken dreams
With all endings, come forth a new beginning
To fulfilling a dream
Above all of that I'll add
God is the truth
The light, and the way
He is the only
Reason I'm here today......................
June 24, 2005

Poem Comments/
Interpretation

THROUGH DARKNESS, TO THE LIGHT

Anybody, everybody
Keep saying, it's a must
History has proven
God's all we can trust
Earthquake, rain flood
Daily shedding the blood
Hurricane Katrina, mudslide
Bible stories they're inside
What's happening now
There's no place to hide
Fathers at odds with sons
Mothers against daughters
It's said more will come
12 days haven't seen the sun
What on earth haven't we done
Hungers left to the poor
At the rate we're going
More of this, and that in store
Population on earth rotten to the core
To come so far, only to go backwards
Somewhere it's been written, go forward
No better time with God to get right
All can ride on this bus
Before days turn into night
Back in time
The word came through
Darkness to the light...................
Oct 15, 2005

Poem Comments/ Interpretation

_____
_____
_____
_____
_____
_____
_____
_____
_____
_____
_____
_____
_____
_____
_____
_____
_____
_____
_____
_____
_____
_____
_____
_____
_____
_____

Send Your Comments/_Interpretations to Mr. Larry "Duce" Cobb_
email address; roxburypoet@yahoo.com

HIS BLESSINGS FOR ME

Once I wouldn't build
On rock the house of my life
Sand was mine's fell with no will
Listening to my own bad advice
Wasn't what God intended
Fact I surrendered spirit was mended
The joy of life and laughter came
Darkness left, light changed the game
For me, God's blessings are all good
Back then I never thought I would
Now I understand
He's had his hand on me
His Blessings for me
The whole world can see..............................
May 4, 2007

Poem Comments/
Interpretation

_____
_____
_____
_____
_____
_____
_____
_____
_____
_____
_____
_____
_____
_____
_____
_____
_____
_____
_____
_____
_____
_____
_____
_____
_____

WHAT'S TO COME NEXT

With our distance
I've found it's true
Love has taken a stance
For the likes of you
Forever is, a long time
To share meetings of the mind
With understanding, we'll be fine
I'll stay yours, just stay mine's
That's not ownership
It's written out of respect
That makes it good, our friendship
To weather, together
What's to come next..............................
Dec 28, 2001

Poem Comments/ Interpretation

_____
_____
_____
_____
_____
_____
_____
_____
_____
_____
_____
_____
_____
_____
_____
_____
_____
_____
_____
_____
_____
_____
_____
_____
_____
_____
_____
_____

Send Your Comments/_Interpretations_ **to Mr. Larry "Duce" Cobb**
email address; roxburypoet@yahoo.com

GO FROM HERE

Where do we go from here
Coming from where we've come
Through all that we've done
In shadow of darkness, from the sun
Where do we go from here
Thoughts of it, drops a tear
For those who didn't reach here
Where do we go from here
Life aint like what's on TV
Paramount actors come back from death
To playing a role in the next movie
That aint how goes with you and me
Where do we go from here
What stories do you now tell
About a chase running to a dry well
Where souls are sold
At a two for one sale
Few survive last stop before Hell
Where do we go from here.................................
Nov 2006

Poem Comments/
Interpretation

AGAIN AND AGAIN

The praying mantis
Has struck, again and again
Once upon a time
You said you loved me
That pillow talk kept saying
What we have will never end
Can you tell, how it happened
Now we're no longer
One another's friend
Talking about a bad thought
Thinking the coast was clear
On a calm ocean, love wasn't there
Wave after wave, it vanished care
From the looks of things
True love never ever lived there
As a flower it grew a courtship
That was a good look at friendship
Good look turned to a bad relationship
Now it's all cards on deck
The call came in, don't wait, abandoned ship
The praying mantis
Has struck again and again
July 23, 2006

Poem Comments/
Interpretation

MORNING

Early morning
Looking and looking
Walking and walking
Searching and searching
For something
But there's nothing to find
Avoiding the warning signs
In slaved within the mind
Being locked in, aint kind
Years and years of wasted time
Long night carried into light of day
Following God's guiding light
As I, they have lost their way
Now, for them everyday, I pray
When I see them all
I see myself back in the day
Where the darkness drove me astray
Today I thank God for changing my
way.........................
Aug 4, 2007

Poem Comments/ Interpretation

_____
_____
_____
_____
_____
_____
_____
_____
_____
_____
_____
_____
_____
_____
_____
_____
_____
_____
_____
_____
_____
_____
_____
_____
_____
_____
_____

Send Your Comments/Interpretations to Mr. Larry "Duce" Cobb
email address; roxburypoet@yahoo.com

TIME WAITS

Time waits on no one
Try saying hold up
A minute, to the morning sun
Forget about it, it aint done
Life's just a minute
Seconds come to be precious
If not in it to win it
It's lost before you begin it
Where's the game plan
When it's not there, get one
To handle life's great demand
Help is found, when this you understand
Many have come, many are gone
Some weak others were strong
A minute doesn't last that long
Life's trials and tribulations
Are lyrics to a happy or sad song
Where will your story belong
Time waits on no one
Try saying hold up
A minute, to the morning sun
Forget about it, it aint done
Nov 29, 2006

Poem Comments/
Interpretation

_____
_____
_____
_____
_____
_____
_____
_____
_____
_____
_____
_____
_____
_____
_____
_____
_____
_____
_____
_____
_____
_____
_____
_____
_____
_____
_____

Send Your Comments/*Interpretations** to Mr. Larry "Duce" Cobb*
email address; roxburypoet@yahoo.com

ANYTHINGS POSSIBLE

I flipped a manhole cover
By any means, made it to the curb
Moving, grooving on the sidewalk
Living life beyond just talk
Where I been, what I've done
As shade, it's been hidden
On the dark side of the sun
No thought, better days would come
Living anywhere with no light
It's hard to see what is right
Staying alive is an everyday fight
Light of hope, doesn't shine so bright
The voice you now hear
Swam here on an ocean of tears
No need to mention how many years
The voice lived with doubts and fears
It's tough standing up
Not falling for anything
Taking care of your business
Being to yourself responsible
In this life, anything is possible
Nov 24, 2006

Poem Comments/ Interpretation

THERE'S NO JOY

Living within
This very dark time
On the throne high, more crime
Stormy troubles For God's sake
Rages on another's mind
Like Sodom and Gomorra
Somewhere back in time
What's so good
Living life dead
Hanging out, with gloom and doom
Sign over head, said and read
Going nowhere, there's plenty of room
It's seen all across the city
So many sitting in self pity
Some care, others just don't care
The reality of the blues
Keeps playing in the inner city
Featuring mom on dope, daddy gone
Not a good look, seeing a broken home
Growth of a child comes to be their own
Soundtrack of this plays on and on
Future of tomorrow, sings a sad song
Sunshine can't find the way here
Only clouds then more clouds
That drop and drop another tear
This stuff goes on year after year
What on earth will it take
So we can straighten this mistake
There's no joy in going to another wake
Oct 20, 2006

Poem Comments/ Interpretation

THE PAIN AND SORROW

Today, we're living in
The belly of the deep
Where we have miles to go
There's no time for us to sleep
Because God has promises
He promises to keep
Are these the last days
Lost souls are walking in a maze
Our nights and our days
These are the ways
The dark has forgotten
The ways of the light
Like Satan's was the one
And you know that aint right
Suicide, genocide, homicide
Between love and hate
There's a great divide
Away from the truth
We just can't hide
Yesterday, today, and tomorrow
Nothing from nothing
Where's nothing to borrow
Look around what do you see
Some can't see, the pain and sorrow

Oct 6, 2005

Poem Comments/ Interpretation

_____
_____
_____
_____
_____
_____
_____
_____
_____
_____
_____
_____
_____
_____
_____
_____
_____
_____
_____
_____
_____
_____
_____
_____
_____

Send Your Comments/_Interpretations_ to Mr. Larry "Duce" Cobb
email address; roxburypoet@yahoo.com

JUST GAZING AT STARS

Eyes been seeing
They keep on seeing
The drowned, drown
They keep on drowning
This crossed my mind
Streets full all the time
Most search for a gold mine
Death after death, changed that time
The Bible speaks of this
Within the pages, bout days of old
Turning back on God, to worship gold
It's different now, so I'm told
The same is welcome, to a lost soul
Block after block, every eye can see
Do you know where your child may be
Daily news become a cold reality
What's going on now, every eye can see
Backwards and downwards aint life
Russian roulette, it's a roll of the dice
Haven't you heard, it aint always so nice
When surrounded by so much bad advice
Being down can lead to death

There's one life to have
It's all you have left
The future of your seed
It's in your hands
Remove yourself, from the jaws of death
Life is all you have left
This writer can sho-nuff speak
Bout it from the cradle to the street
Mine's yesterday, your's today
God knows it's truth, what I speak
Forecast ahead here's a peek
I've lived on both sides, of the bars
Home always seem to be, somewhere beyond Mars
Who said it aint lonely, anywhere behind bars
At night I would escape, just gazing at stars
Jan 18, 2006

Poem Comments/ Interpretation

_____
_____
_____
_____
_____
_____
_____
_____
_____
_____
_____
_____
_____
_____
_____
_____
_____
_____
_____
_____
_____
_____
_____
_____
_____

Send Your Comments/Interpretations to Mr. Larry "Duce" Cobb
email address; roxburypoet@yahoo.com

WHICH I NOW WALK

We've all heard
Over and over again
The sounds of these words
Somewhere the blues singers
Lives to write songs they sing
Of an eagle who broke it's wing
Our thinking and our thoughts
Allows bells of freedom to ring
Those are the keys
To opening freedoms locks
To touch the untouchable stars
Up, up, high, high above
Self imposed prison bars
No man nor woman
Can ever set you free
From where ever you're at
To where ever you pray to be
Sad to say some of us
May not make it there
To some freedom, it's an odd job

Because for others
The task is to damn hard
To ask, knock, and seek
Help from the Almighty God
As it's been written and told
The betterment of one's self
It's soothing to the soul
More precious than
A mountain of choice gold
Through my testimony it's shown
From myself, my freedom I stole
Chose a life of a mass bandit
Behind bars I landed
No, no this wasn't
The way I planned it
Chance for self, never gave
Trials and tribulations
Whichever rescued or saved
Now freedoms brand new road
Which I now walk, God has paved
Nov 25, 2006

Poem Comments/ Interpretation

RED ALERT, DANGER, DANGER

Now, now what you do
Don't think it's brand new
It wasn't put in place
By your crew, but it seems so new
Well son, hear this
To be an O.G there's risk
Getting pass death's last kiss
When you don't make it
Like they say, you're one we miss
Now get to this
OG's start was like yours
Helping by opening and closing doors
Here and there doing hood chores
Don't think, the game's all yours

Mothers, fathers, aunts and uncles
Played life's dangerous games
Some made it, others to never to be the same
Aint that a crying shame
Life offers two things for sure
One's sad, the other is a precious treasure
They happen to be Life and Death
Before you may choose
Last stop on the block
Giving the only life you have left
None of my homies, returned from death
Here's the question upon your head
Have you heard what the old folks said
You ever see crabs in a basket
As you make your climb to the top
Jealousy will put you in a casket
Sometimes it's a friend, other times it's a stranger
RED ALERT, DANGER, DANGER
May 8, 2003,

Poem Comments/ Interpretation

_____
_____
_____
_____
_____
_____
_____
_____
_____
_____
_____
_____
_____
_____
_____
_____
_____
_____
_____
_____
_____
_____
_____
_____

BELONGED TO YOU

What once was
Doesn't seem to be
Love's been set free
From where it used to be
To roam far away
Beyond where it was to stay
Nowhere to be found today
If we could only bring back yesterday
Silence, moment of silence
As I send God this prayer
For his personal alliance
Don't let love be silenced
Cover it with wings that spread
Where lives are being mislead
Truth's always good for the head
Lie after lie is an unmade bed
Good times gone, hard to come back
That's just a loveable fact
It's the weight that broke
The story, that broke the camels back
Water under the bridge
Is long, long been gone
Here you got to be strong
When the love of love stories, goes wrong
That CD more than once listened to
Playing within my heart
Just isn't getting through
To my heart, that once belonged to you
June 23, 2004

Poem Comments/ Interpretation

_____
_____
_____
_____
_____
_____
_____
_____
_____
_____
_____
_____
_____
_____
_____
_____
_____
_____
_____
_____
_____
_____
_____
_____

Send Your Comments/Interpretations to Mr. Larry "Duce" Cobb
email address; roxburypoet@yahoo.com

ALL ALONE

Round the corner
Down many alleys
Been down through
Many, many valleys
Giving and receiving
What's to get and give
Where lost souls
Still now live
There's not much room
Between gloom and doom
It continues to pull
On the minds
Tears that fall
It continues to pull
On the minds
That are empty or full
Are you living
Last house on the left
Falling, and sliding down
Just before coming, of death
Work a blessing
Or live a curse
Which do you choose
To be the first

The well you drink from
God knows, will quench your thirst
Looking at my past
Through my own eyes
Opportunity Satan denies
The promise maker and faker
Story teller, of all lies
He'll creep up in your life
You'll stand a better chance
At a crap game, rolling dice
He'll deceive to please, then leave
After to him, you've given your life
Beware!!!! Where you get your advice
Tears that fall
When no one is watching
Only God hears that call
When the strong grow weak
Falling and sliding down
Far beneath and below your peak
Tears of fear, tears of doubt
Belong to you, it's your own
Sitting in darkness, all alone.........
June 9, 2006

Poem Comments/ Interpretation

Send Your Comments/*Interpretations* **to Mr. Larry "Duce" Cobb**
email address; roxburypoet@yahoo.com

WHO AM I

That drug I kicked
Could've left me dead
It messed up my life
I never could stay ahead
Always trying to fight it
Mind said, it felt to good
It even made me say
Rob my homies, from the hood
The drugs always talked to me
No doubt, I'd pay attention
Never saying, yo, yo Juice
Slow down on your addiction
Who am I.......
Hurry up, come get me
Before it gets to damn late
You know every morning
Together we have a date
You better get up out of bed
The drug said, get to me quick
What I got, will do the trick
Before your ass is on "E" and sick
No need to brush your teeth
No need to wash your face
Arrive at my house, come on
Where broken dreams, has a place

Who am I.........
The drug speak
Just get yourself to me
So I can make you feel okay
If not there's more in store
To the makings of a hard day
That's how it comes out
When anyone takes me in
Drugs spoke, no one controls me
At the end of the day, I always win
All through the day
My heart says, Please God, stay my friend
Who am I........
Who am I...... Another voice spoke
Who am I.......
May 5, 2007

Poem Comments/
Interpretation

_____
_____
_____
_____
_____
_____
_____
_____
_____
_____
_____
_____
_____
_____
_____
_____
_____
_____
_____
_____
_____
_____
_____
_____
_____
_____
_____

OUT REACHING HAND

All wonder about
How the rich got rich
No one speaks about
How the poor became poor
Outdoors, things colder than before
Family and friends disappear
Strangers pass by, they stare
Never thinking, this could be them
Point of view, the poor sees no care
Where hope was blown away on thin air
Was it a lost love
Maybe a broken dream
Making streams of tears
Into rivers of pain, over the years
While drowning in an ocean, of doubts and fears
Down in there, it's tough getting up
Living in memories of days gone by
Did you ever think, they've been asking God
To change their way into luck
The past has a way of keeping us stuck
Subway stations, doorways, cups, you can hear
Change, do you have some to spare

Just to live in another day, of despair
Not many stop, to hear words they share
Remove the fear, ask how it got this way
To understand there's a price to pay
For things done yesterday, and today
Tomorrow's lessons are given here today
Then we'll come to understand
A life of such great demand
Our best laid plan, finished in a trash can
Wouldn't you want, an out reached hand.....
Feb 10, 2006

Poem Comments/ Interpretation

_____
_____
_____
_____
_____
_____
_____
_____
_____
_____
_____
_____
_____
_____
_____
_____
_____
_____
_____
_____
_____
_____
_____
_____
_____
_____
_____
_____

Send Your Comments/_Interpretations_ to Mr. _Larry "Duce" Cobb_
email address; roxburypoet@yahoo.com

CHOOSE WELL TO LIVE

Same as Mama's
Grits in the pot
Heat from the streets
It's getting to damn hot
Many search and search
For a place to hide
Then there's some others
That keep a gun by their side
Some haven't got a future
To look forward to
What's written above
Is it happening to you
Don't let them die
Hopes, wishes, a dream
While they're in Brick Cities
That hard, cold, and mean
The old folks said
Keep your head up, Son
Life's happy and sad
Get some living done
Your mother, my mother

Dropped this on us
For us to hold on to
In us they only trust
They made the sacrifice
So they could survive
All so we would
Make better of our lives
Some don't think so
To the world you have much to give
It's decision time
Choose well to live and live.....
April 9, 1999

Poem Comments/ Interpretation

_____
_____
_____
_____
_____
_____
_____
_____
_____
_____
_____
_____
_____
_____
_____
_____
_____
_____
_____
_____
_____
_____
_____
_____
_____
_____
_____

Send Your Comments/Interpretations to Mr. Larry "Duce" Cobb
email address; roxburypoet@yahoo.com

DREAMS THEY SOUGHT

Bout the street soldier
No matter what, they had souls
Whether in Heaven, or delivered to Hell
Some of these stories saved others
Profit was gained by a newspaper sale
That told of a mothers Angel that fell
Serious, dangerous work put in
Over and over , again and again
Whether it be a enemy or a friend
In to deep to get out, of what they got in
Ticket to ride on, got canceled
Some to many wasn't trying to hear
No good advice or to be counseled
The verdict was life got canceled
Living on wild side, it's tough to tame
The Government, society shoulder the blame
Name and name after another name
Their demise didn't change the game
The block remembers the friendship
Of a shining stars fatal dip
Memories continues to ride a ghost ship
Mother's understanding lost it's grip
Gone to a world of no return
From this and that
There's much to learn
They taught through wars they fought
From the block to dreams they sought
Dec 29, 2006

Poem Comments/
Interpretation

_____
_____
_____
_____
_____
_____
_____
_____
_____
_____
_____
_____
_____
_____
_____
_____
_____
_____
_____
_____
_____
_____
_____
_____
_____
_____

Send Your Comments/*Interpretations* **to Mr. Larry "Duce" Cobb**
email address; roxburypoet@yahoo.com

COLORS OF THE RAINBOW

Within the colors of the rainbow
A voice is heard
That voice, all want to know
To the future
Which way shall we go
The worlds full of pollution
Good seems to be an illusion
Death after death, destruction
It's a problem with no solution
The children are running wild
Adults living in denial
Now it seems it hurts to smile
While God is keeping it on file
Which way shall we go
To the future
That all want to know
A voice is heard
Within the colors
Of the rainbow
March 23, 2008

Poem Comments/ Interpretation

HOPE IN SIGHT

Twilight,
Came before night
Darkness kept, hope in sight
Intertwining shadows moved
Between the hoods street lights
Things done, wasn't always right
What's worth having and keeping
Morning, noon and every night
God knows, it's worth a fight
Here we continue to stand
Keeping the dream, from falling
Into the nearest trash can
Some understand, we understand
The hell with living, out of a trash can
Twilight,
Came before night
Darkness kept, hope in sight
Feb 15, 2008

Poem Comments/ Interpretation

_____
_____
_____
_____
_____
_____
_____
_____
_____
_____
_____
_____
_____
_____
_____
_____
_____
_____
_____
_____
_____
_____
_____
_____
_____
_____

THE PLACE TO

Since God
Set me free
Those old streets
Keep calling me
The way it is now
Aint what it use to be
Code of absolute silence
Got lost along the way
Betrayal stole the balance
Listen, carefully listen
Now nothing done in silence
A road paved with temptation
Takes a hell of a toll on a soul
Step away from self destruction
God's the place to receive salvation
May 13, 2007

Poem Comments/ Interpretation

_____
_____
_____
_____
_____
_____
_____
_____
_____
_____
_____
_____
_____
_____
_____
_____
_____
_____
_____
_____
_____
_____
_____
_____
_____
_____
_____
_____

Send Your Comments/Interpretations to Mr. Larry "Duce" Cobb
email address; roxburypoet@yahoo.com

CHANGE

Believe it or not
When good is sought
Something is done
Get with it, cast in your lot
Leave behind, what was
To get where you pray to be
Change is, hope unseen
Something must die
Before fulfilling a dream
To some
This sounds strange
Staying the same
Aint change................................
March 29, 2008

Poem Comments/
Interpretation

_____
_____
_____
_____
_____
_____
_____
_____
_____
_____
_____
_____
_____
_____
_____
_____
_____
_____
_____
_____
_____
_____
_____
_____
_____
_____
_____

Send Your Comments/Interpretations to Mr. Larry "Duce" Cobb
email address; roxburypoet@yahoo.com

NEVER-EVER BEEN PLAYED

Walked passed
Window covered by glass
Stopped and watched
Reflections that passed
If you don't wake up
You will stay sleep
Chasing after dreams
You'll never ever keep
Trying to catch
A time, that's lost
Is like winning a game
That's never ever been played
Jan 19, 2008
March 29, 2008
Nov 24, 2007

Poem Comments/ Interpretation

THE STREETS

The streets
Continue to flood
From streams to rivers
To an ocean of blood
The streets
Have painted a picture
Fear adds, to the measure
Not one of pleasure
The streets
What was then, now it's gone
The missing list grows long
Open eyes see the wrong
Young ones stand, cup in hand
Old ones fallen under great demand
Losing understanding, to understand
The streets
Despair walks on two feet
Where the lost stand in defeat
Hunger hunts for food to eat
The streets
Wine, coke, and dope
Takes away life's will to cope
It's left behind, that thing called hope
The streets
Nowhere to turn
Lifes lessons we earn
Out here there's much to learn
The Streets.........
May 12, 2006

Poem Comments/ Interpretation

_____
_____
_____
_____
_____
_____
_____
_____
_____
_____
_____
_____
_____
_____
_____
_____
_____
_____
_____
_____
_____
_____
_____
_____
_____
_____

Send Your Comments/Interpretations to Mr. Larry "Duce" Cobb
email address; roxburypoet@yahoo.com

FOR THE BUS I RODE

Fire, Ice, Ashes
Wind blown dust
Anger and danger rode the bus
There was no room for care
It didn't ride with us
How we lived our lives, began with a must
These were the days, of our lives
Before sundown or after sunrise
A tear formed, in corner of eyes
Because the book of life
Closed down on many lives
Some to many I knew
Others never known
Name spoken from the past
Pictures of them being shown
The path of life we choose, was our own
Now riding the bus at times, I feel alone
Where no one seems to know your name
So many different things, changed the game
What we did to ourselves, was a crying shame
Whichever way it went down
This thing touched others
If it was wrong, it wasn't dismissed
Not even coming from a blood brother
Our life style brought tears and pain
To more than just one somebody's mother
Forgive me, for the bus I rode, my brother
March 1, 2006

Poem Comments/
Interpretation

AGONY OF DEFEAT

The heat, from the streets
Continues to light the flame
There's no need to wonder
Bout the changing of the game
What use to be, lost its fun
Cause the Feds, got-em on the run
Hiding like shade does from the sun
Watch what you do, and how it's done
In the beginning
It was all about the winning
Now in every other hood
The fight over the hood, we're losing
Where we roamed, in the concrete jungle
Running fast as gavel
To keep life you had to rumble
No understanding about living life humble
It's a desert without a well
Even an Angel came here, and fell
Newspapers, what do they tell
Sign post read, welcome to Hell
Teddy bears, pictures and flowers
Continue to line up on the streets
Heat makes waves in the street
Thrill of victory
Meets agony of defeat..........
April 7, 2006

Poem Comments/
Interpretation

_____
_____
_____
_____
_____
_____
_____
_____
_____
_____
_____
_____
_____
_____
_____
_____
_____
_____
_____
_____
_____
_____
_____
_____
_____
_____
_____
_____
_____

Send Your Comments/Interpretations to Mr. Larry "Duce" Cobb
email address; roxburypoet@yahoo.com

THAT WILL BE PAID

These are desperate times
Stress continues to creep
Up and through, on more minds
Are these the coming of the ending signs
It's broken many to a few
By the things we go through
Has it come to live with you
It's turned up, that old desperation
With a friend, whose name is temptation
Churches continue to holler, holler salvation
Living right here, that's hard to hear
There aint no hiding, from this damn nation
Where the weak are getting weaker
Dreams keep disappearing, on the seeker
Politicians say help is on the way
Standing on a soap box, with a loud speaker
Where the quicksand continues to get deeper
Living in the shade, aint so sunny
Street side seeing, the other
Money to where there's no money
It aint changed, bad joke aint funny
Quite a mess we've made
The Gospel's now, it's man made
For this there's a price
That will be paid............
April 6, 2006

Poem Comments/ Interpretation

_____
_____
_____
_____
_____
_____
_____
_____
_____
_____
_____
_____
_____
_____
_____
_____
_____
_____
_____
_____
_____
_____
_____
_____
_____
_____

FROM THE OLD DAYS

Seven different days
History of violence touched
Seven families, seven different ways
Quite a change, from the old days
The record book was broken
Homicide rolling up on high
Where a young life, stopped to die
Only answer to the question, is why
God please hear, a mother and families help cry
Evil keeps on pushing the good
On every street corner, in the hood
Respect for life, aint to the good
For God sake, what happened to the hood
Lost the way, and belief in salvation
Sodom and Gomorrah, fell under temptation
Look around, see all the self destruction
Respect for life, will it return from vacation
Seven different days
History of violence touched
Seven families, seven different ways
Quite a change, from the old days........
May 9, 2006

Poem Comments/
Interpretation

THE GRAY CLOUD

Beneath the gray cloud
Siren sounds, hauntingly loud
Race to save the young and proud
Who dwell beneath the gray cloud
Will understanding arrive in time
Are these the coming of the ending signs
Misunderstandings divide great minds
Will understanding arrive in time
History has shown who you really are
Ancestors navigated oceans by the stars
You've lost control, not knowing who you are
Mothers prayers sent to God beyond the stars
How many more must we lose
Being played by Satan, being his fools
Past great minds played by the rules
God's book and words, are our tools to use
How many more must we lose
Believe it or not, we are connected
Truth is, yall are being misdirected
I understand, you don't like being corrected
Stop, look and listen who's being disrespected
Do you know who you serve
Will understanding arrive in time
Are these the coming, of ending signs
Misunderstandings, divide great minds
Will understanding, arrive in time
Beneath the gray cloud
Siren sounds, hauntingly loud
Race to save the young and proud
Who will dwell beneath the gray cloud...

Oct 5, 2006

Poem Comments/ Interpretation

_____
_____
_____
_____
_____
_____
_____
_____
_____
_____
_____
_____
_____
_____
_____
_____
_____
_____
_____
_____
_____
_____
_____
_____
_____
_____

Send Your Comments/*Interpretations* to Mr. Larry "Duce" Cobb
email address; roxburypoet@yahoo.com

SAVED BY GOD

Truth will hurt
Beneath the dirt
Before the removal
Of the out house
I was born there
Taught there to care
About giving and receiving
All get their share
Words to the foolish
Beware, beware
I've shaken hands with revelation
Now living in BosBean town
Thanking God for removing that old temptation
Cream rises from lowdown
Those things which destroy, the youth in our
nation
How does that there sound
I was saved by God and his salvation…..
Coming from southern Georgia town

Family came here to chill
Against my own will
Fighting the clan, never sat still
Grew up some living off Blue Hill
As I write this now
I see my best friend
He's gone now, still hearing him saying
We're from the Hill
Where we never work
And never ever will
Down under the south
That was then, this is now
Living changed that, I'll show how
Growing old wasn't in the plan
Then I misunderstood
Now I understand
Out of it I grew to be a man
Like I said, growing old wasn't in the plan
As you see before you I stand
May 22, 2005

Poem Comments/ Interpretation

ABOVE UNDERGROUND

Stairway to Heaven
Expressway to Hell
Which one of these stories
Does your story tell
About the good and bad
Of a dream you once had
There's no two ways about it
It was either good or very bad
Is it half full or half empty
What's in your hand, the glass
Tough look at the past
In the middle, being an outcast
What does it look like, the world
Watching, watching it pass by
No winners when you don't try
Truth bout the mirror, it doesn't lie
What you standing there for
A broken spirit, hurts to the core
Opportunity is knocking, open the door

What you standing there for
Otherwise move out of the way
Life's a game you got to play
No pity if you want
To stay where you stay
Moving forward not backwards
It's different from back in the day
It never ever stops, the grind
Here and now make good of your time
Did you hear, so and so lost their damn mind
For no one does it wait...time
Much is in the lost and found
Hear the spoken word, and the sound
The living dead
Wander and wander above underground......
Sept 30, 2006

Poem Comments/
Interpretation

_____
_____
_____
_____
_____
_____
_____
_____
_____
_____
_____
_____
_____
_____
_____
_____
_____
_____
_____
_____
_____
_____
_____
_____
_____
_____
_____
_____

STICK AROUND

Try hard
Once again
So better
Fits itself in
It's gone
Days of old
No reward
In old stories told
There's a need
To survive
Change comes
By changing our lives
Don't be
A modern day slave
By running and working to
An early, early grave
Death offers
Lessons to learn
Through living
Blessings you earn
Life has many
A mystery
Stick around to write your own history............
Oct 31, 2002

Poem Comments/ Interpretation

_____
_____
_____
_____
_____
_____
_____
_____
_____
_____
_____
_____
_____
_____
_____
_____
_____
_____
_____
_____
_____
_____
_____
_____
_____
_____
_____

AINT WHAT IT USE TO BE

Since God
Saved and set me free
Them there, old streets
Keep on calling me
Since God
Saved and set me free
The way it is now
Aint what it use to be
Nothing done in silence
That got lost along the way
Betrayal broke the balance
To the code, of absolute silence
Now anger, and danger in the air
Place where tempers flair
There's a war within the minds here
Some do, others just don't care
Between hope, and despair
On any God given night
Beneath urban street lights
Cries, gunshots are heard
Did childs mother get the word
Satan's sitting back in delight
Son or daughter lost their birthright
Madness marches on
Where it was, happiness now gone
Who can say, what written is wrong
Another community, writes a sad song
Them there, old streets
Keep on calling me
The way it is now
Aint what it use to be.........
Nov 2, 2005

Poem Comments/ Interpretation

_____
_____
_____
_____
_____
_____
_____
_____
_____
_____
_____
_____
_____
_____
_____
_____
_____
_____
_____
_____
_____
_____
_____
_____

Send Your Comments/Interpretations to Mr. Larry "Duce" Cobb
email address; roxburypoet@yahoo.com

GHETTO PAIN

United souls
Come together
As those of
The same feather
To help one another
Through life's
Calm and stormy weather
We are the link
Throughout the chain
With ears to hear
The dripping of the rain
Where its heard and felt
Ghetto pain.......
July 20, 2006

Poem Comments/ Interpretation

_____
_____
_____
_____
_____
_____
_____
_____
_____
_____
_____
_____
_____
_____
_____
_____
_____
_____
_____
_____
_____
_____
_____
_____
_____
_____

THANK YOU......GOD

God, first I'd like to
Thank you and thank you
For the many, many times
You've helped me through
Without your loving care
Left to me, I wouldn't be here
You've given and granted me
So much of the love you share
When times seemed very dark
Doubt and fear came to move
Today I am not afraid
Because your light lit the spark
I walk no longer in the dark
God thank you, thank you
For holding me up
To make it through
Thank you, thank you God...........
April 25, 2007

Poem Comments/ Interpretation

_____
_____
_____
_____
_____
_____
_____
_____
_____
_____
_____
_____
_____
_____
_____
_____
_____
_____
_____
_____
_____
_____
_____
_____
_____

THE BOOK

Behind the wall
Where the falling, fall
Place named forbidden
So much has been hidden
Beyond the eyes of proof
Time and time again it's shown
God revealing to us the truth
Greed throughout humanity
Has gone too far
It's leaving road kill
Served bloody, and raw
It's so bad, nothing seen
Are you left in awe
By what the eyes just saw
Love stepped off
Sign posted, gone on long vacation
Leaving far behind
Worldwide temptation
Hood to hood, nation to nation
Who here hasn't read
The book of revelation...............
Oct 7, 2005

Poem Comments/ Interpretation

_____
_____
_____
_____
_____
_____
_____
_____
_____
_____
_____
_____
_____
_____
_____
_____
_____
_____
_____
_____
_____
_____
_____
_____
_____
_____

Send Your Comments/_Interpretations_ to Mr. Larry "Duce" Cobb
email address; roxburypoet@yahoo.com

STORIES TO MEMORIES

Stories to memories
Memories to stories
Have a way
To telling of true stories
From lies and falling from glory
What you read, and what you hear
God knows
It's truth to these stories
In the beginning
Long before the sinning
Life was for the winning
Somewhere it changed, to losing
Running so fast, to a life ending
More than once
I was a prisoner
Champion of a lost cause
No respect
For the makers of the laws
It wasn't a fairy tale
Like the wizard of OZ
Near death for a hopeless cause
Caught in a trap
The young ones continued rap
Freedom came for me through a nap
Awakening out of a dream of dreams
Couldn't sleep away time, on a nap
Caught in a trap
Stories to memories
Memories to stories.....
June 22, 2005

Poem Comments/ Interpretation

_____
_____
_____
_____
_____
_____
_____
_____
_____
_____
_____
_____
_____
_____
_____
_____
_____
_____
_____
_____
_____
_____
_____
_____
_____
_____
_____

WE WILL TOUCHDOWN

Does anybody know
Or can someone show
Which way
True values went
Given to us
By God, Heaven sent
As it was nothings the same
Together we shoulder the blame
How on earth did we change the game
Some scream, others holler
From the ball and chain
Tightly fit around the collar
Some scream, others holler
It's the kind of stuff
Making life rough
When values disappear
The one's that use to be here
What happened to go forward
For all eyes to see
It looks like we're going backwards
We are going down, down
Any farther
Hell is where we will touchdown.........
May 1, 2003

Poem Comments/ Interpretation

_____
_____
_____
_____
_____
_____
_____
_____
_____
_____
_____
_____
_____
_____
_____
_____
_____
_____
_____
_____
_____
_____
_____
_____
_____
_____
_____
_____
_____

Send Your Comments/Interpretations to Mr. Larry "Duce" Cobb
email address; roxburypoet@yahoo.com

THE VISIT

The visit
The address is,
One fear, two doubt
House stands on, street court
Many there praying for a way out
The reason here you can't erase
Being down, there's much to face
The loss of life, you can't replace
Self love will lose its taste
You or others aren't first or last
Who have walked and ran down this path
Many to a few just won't last
To share with grandchild about the past
Don't think a half a second
That it was easy street for me
I thank God
I'm here so you can see
I made it out
From where I use to be
I pray God Blesses you
As he did for me
In my thinking, there was a move
My thoughts started to improve
As you know, I knew
No winners, there you lose
Now I'm in the flow
With God's stuff....I can't lose
March 30, 2005

Poem Comments/ Interpretation

_____
_____
_____
_____
_____
_____
_____
_____
_____
_____
_____
_____
_____
_____
_____
_____
_____
_____
_____
_____
_____
_____
_____
_____
_____
_____

Send Your Comments/Interpretations to Mr. Larry "Duce" Cobb
email address; roxburypoet@yahoo.com

INFERNO.......

Inferno
Ferno ......
No
That's that place
Mama said, son don't go
Point of no return
Hells inferno
You won't meet the wizard of OZ
So fight for your freedom
Don't be a prisoner of the cause
Good practice is, God's laws
No inferno, you've been told
It has no joy or love
That stuffs not even thought of
Love belongs to God up above
No inferno
Has never ever been cool
It has only one rule
That's to put the heat
To a damn fool
Gloom and doom
Await the lives
That fill each and every room
The inferno
It's gloom and doom
June 12, 2005

Poem Comments/
Interpretation

_____
_____
_____
_____
_____
_____
_____
_____
_____
_____
_____
_____
_____
_____
_____
_____
_____
_____
_____
_____
_____
_____
_____
_____
_____
_____

Send Your Comments/_Interpretations_ to Mr. Larry "Duce" Cobb
email address; roxburypoet@yahoo.com

BEFORE ONLOOKERS EYES

We rise, we rise
The things put down
Down beneath the ground
That broke, and shattered lives
Like surround sound
The stories, much is left out
Where lives intertwine
Surviving beyond a drought
Standing at the door
Of fear and much doubt
Then it was a bad attitude
Chances with life
Lost love for self
No care for anyone else
Giving up freedom
Living in bondage
Endless chase for drugs
Love swept under the rug

Now this is
A better attitude
Thankful new life was given
Love for self found
Care given to others
Thanking God, free at last
So many of us
Didn't live beyond the past........
From ashes to ashes
Above dust to dust
As the Phoenix
That belief, belong to us
As it rose, we rise
Short stopping our demise
Before onlookers eyes
We rose, we rise
Now we still rise
Jan 14, 2008

Poem Comments/ Interpretation

_____
_____
_____
_____
_____
_____
_____
_____
_____
_____
_____
_____
_____
_____
_____
_____
_____
_____
_____
_____
_____
_____
_____
_____
_____
_____
_____
_____
_____

Send Your Comments/Interpretations to Mr. Larry "Duce" Cobb
email address; roxburypoet@yahoo.com

A CHILDS LOVE CAN DO

Through the eyes
Of a child
Hope was seen
Wearing a smile
I've journeyed
A many a mile
Learning the meaning
To love and much care
From then to now
It's a breath of fresh air
Bright sun, skies clear blue
It's amazing to what
A Childs love can do.........

2007

Poem Comments/ Interpretation

_____
_____
_____
_____
_____
_____
_____
_____
_____
_____
_____
_____
_____
_____
_____
_____
_____
_____
_____
_____
_____
_____
_____
_____
_____
_____

Send Your Comments/Interpretations to Mr. Larry "Duce" Cobb
email address; roxburypoet@yahoo.com

BAD MEANING GOOD

Bad meaning good
It's something misunderstood
The understanding of it
Lives around the way, the hood
Giving to life
The low down reality
Within the many storms
Through another tragedy
Negative after negative
Takes the water and the fruit
God knows
He had something bad to give
Bad meaning good
Is alive to live
Baby child start out
Knowing nothing about
Those things, called fear and doubt
He's got to stand out
Living up against a wall

Of many, many bricks
Didn't know daddy was
Sentenced to life at age six
That was the very beginning
Of life's many, many tricks
At tender age of seven
Baby child loses, Mama to Heaven
Living in a whirlwind by age eleven
Left alone, but with good advice
Living with pimps and hustlers was his device
Everything, became a roll of the dice
Hell of a way to start off in life
I'm talking about, no other choice
From the start, he had to play the game
What was to be ,will never ever be the same
Mean to survive
From then to now, he's not ashamed
Aint no other way to finish
He's got to play the game
In a very cold world
I got to end this
To stand down
To hand it up
To Menace………
July 25, 2006

Poem Comments/
Interpretation

_____
_____
_____
_____
_____
_____
_____
_____
_____
_____
_____
_____
_____
_____
_____
_____
_____
_____
_____
_____
_____
_____
_____
_____

Send Your Comments/Interpretations to Mr. Larry "Duce" Cobb
email address; roxburypoet@yahoo.com

STATING

Now is the time
Don't waste a good mind
Living deaf, dumb and blind
That's the truth about the grind
Camel's back broke, caused by weight
There's no time, time doesn't wait
Right now, everything's at stake
True to the game, this aint no mistake
Empire's rise, big or small
From start to the end they all fall
What happened to the rule book
Stating, all for one, and one for all
May 24, 2006

.

Poem Comments/
Interpretation

_____
_____
_____
_____
_____
_____
_____
_____
_____
_____
_____
_____
_____
_____
_____
_____
_____
_____
_____
_____
_____
_____
_____
_____
_____
_____

Send Your Comments/*Interpretations* to Mr. Larry "Duce" Cobb
email address; roxburypoet@yahoo.com

TOGETHER WE CAN

The winds of change
In the niche of time
Has come
To some, it's strange
Wanting better
To be done
Betterment for all
Each one will grow
Beneath the sun
Together we can
United we will stand
For changing, our future plan
Change is hard, to come by
Being willing, changes the lie
Stand fast, allow change to come by
So we can heal
Beyond a crooked mistake
Is what it takes, for God's sake……..
Written for Governor Patrick Deval
Nov 4, 2006

Poem Comments/ Interpretation

MUCH LOVE.......

Many have come
To where you stand
Only to fail
By not having a future plan
Within your journey, and actions
There's no question
You've come to understand
What's between a plan, and no plan........
Many, many blessings
Very, very best of wishes
From your Auntie, Joanie
Much love, and more kisses.............
May 12, 2007

Poem Comments/ Interpretation

THOSE THINGS CALLED

This may not
The doors of Heaven
Life's a crap game
Winners and losers
Wish for seven or eleven
Lack of wisdom
No knowledge, no understanding
Voices and stories they tell
No water is in a dried up well
The tree, God said don't eat there
They did, that's how we got here
Where one to the other, shows no care
Has love of love vanished around here
Who needs a napkin for the next tear
Time and time, again and again
The grave diggers continue to dig
Space for another somebody to fit in
God knows it's just got to stop
18, 17, 16, 15, 14, 13
Never ever got a living chance
To fulfilling a promising dream
Genocide is, a designers scheme
Daily what's seen, aint a daydream
The lost of the lost generation
Show no signs, for God's salvation
It's happening straight cross the nation
When hopes gone, here comes
Those things called, Death and Destruction
Jan 30, 2007

Poem Comments/
Interpretation

_____
_____
_____
_____
_____
_____
_____
_____
_____
_____
_____
_____
_____
_____
_____
_____
_____
_____
_____
_____
_____
_____
_____
_____
_____

Send Your Comments/Interpretations to Mr. Larry "Duce" Cobb
email address; roxburypoet@yahoo.com

THE LADY, AND THE MAN

I have felt
The sounds of love
By no means
Was it from above
Many, many times
It's nothing, but a word
Surely it's been written
Love's an action word
The limits of love
Never ever had an end
Wherever it starts
That's where it begins
Being a lover's one thing
Important, being a friend
Hearts of hearts come together
Touching the other with no end
Love doesn't live in quicksand
When it's given, and received
On top of a mountain it stands
When there's love between
The lady and the man.........
April 26, 2007

Poem Comments/
Interpretation

AMONGST THE STARS

The beauty of
Ebony eyes
Touches a heart
At sun rise
To see blackness
In eyes that are alive
A Diamond, a Ruby, a Pearl
Let no one deny, look in the eyes
You've come so very far
To where you came to be
All knew they had to raise the bar
Because you were given by God
To shine in the sky, amongst the stars...................
May 3, 2007

Poem Comments/
Interpretation

_____
_____
_____
_____
_____
_____
_____
_____
_____
_____
_____
_____
_____
_____
_____
_____
_____
_____
_____
_____
_____
_____
_____
_____
_____
_____

HOW'D IT GET AWAY

Once closer than most
Sharing last piece of toast
Care vanished on thin air
As if to have seen a ghost
Together, touched a revelation
Now feeling the makings of rejection
To and from a broken connection
This picture, needs an inspection
Once we carried the olive branch
Delivered to us, by the dove
Our love of the others love
How's it get away, our love..........................
Feb 3, 2007

Poem Comments/ Interpretation

BURNT OUT SUPER STAR

You got to come
A long way
To get this far
Beyond what was done
Along the way
To being a superstar
So if you aint there
You're playing your life
More than a little, over par
Broken dreams of
A burnt out superstar.......................................
Feb 3, 2007

Poem Comments/
Interpretation

_____
_____
_____
_____
_____
_____
_____
_____
_____
_____
_____
_____
_____
_____
_____
_____
_____
_____
_____
_____
_____
_____
_____
_____

Send Your Comments/Interpretations to Mr. Larry "Duce" Cobb
email address; roxburypoet@yahoo.com

HAVE SOME FUN

My, my, my
The rising sun
Chance to live
Again has come
Pray, Love, Work
And have some
fun...
Feb 6, 2007

Poem Comments/
Interpretation

_____
_____
_____
_____
_____
_____
_____
_____
_____
_____
_____
_____
_____
_____
_____
_____
_____
_____
_____
_____
_____
_____
_____
_____

BEYOND THE EYES

Has anyone seen
What use to be
Love, Truth, Peace and Harmony
Did it vanished, and disappear
In the deep, deep blue sea
Will it ever come to rise again
To remove the gloom of darkness
So the sun will rise
To shine to hearts
Beyond the eyes...................
May 14, 2006

Poem Comments/ Interpretation

WITHIN THE LIGHT

The dream of you
Which came to me
On many past nights
Upon my awakening
You were gone
Cornered in a maze
The search was on
Within many dreams
The hunt for you was strong
Somehow, someway, it was built
A lasting bond
That's the dream
Here's the reality
Appearing beyond the dream
Loyalty which stays, and stays
Within the light
Of greater days.....................................
July 18, 2003

Poem Comments/
Interpretation

_____
_____
_____
_____
_____
_____
_____
_____
_____
_____
_____
_____
_____
_____
_____
_____
_____
_____
_____
_____
_____
_____

Send Your Comments/Interpretations to Mr. Larry "Duce" Cobb
email address; roxburypoet@yahoo.com

A PHAT LOVE

With your love
I'll never go on a diet
Not since
You've allowed me to try it
The love you give
Has made my life very fat
And I must say,
I like it like that
On me
You can pour
All your love
And I'll like that even more..........
July 11, 1993

Poem Comments/ Interpretation

NEVER EVER DERAIL

You've stuck with me
Through so many times
When it was thick and thin
With you I knew we would win
You're the pillow I leaned on
Little did you know
You helped me to be strong
We're the glue, to our bond
Together, the wind and the sail
On the water only to float
Where others came just to fail
What we got, may it never ever derail...........
Sept 16, 2007

Poem Comments/ Interpretation

HOLD STILL

Hold still
Let me talk to you
Bout just how I feel
These here, are words
To no other, do I reveal
Many come, many gone
The love you give, and give
Happens to be your magic wand
Touching me to the point
To writing you another love song
It's keeping us within a groove
What's shared between us
To no other, do we have to prove
Hold still, just don't move............
Sept 14, 15, 2007

Poem Comments/
Interpretation

_____
_____
_____
_____
_____
_____
_____
_____
_____
_____
_____
_____
_____
_____
_____
_____
_____
_____
_____
_____
_____
_____
_____
_____
_____
_____

Send Your Comments/_Interpretations_ to Mr. Larry "Duce" Cobb
email address; roxburypoet@yahoo.com

TO A BLESSING

Be blessed, be healed, to prosper
There's more added to the roster
To avoiding Satan, the great imposter
The buyer and the taker of a soul
Haven't you heard, don't worship gold
It was written and seen in
The Greatest Story Ever Told
That was then, this is now
No difference here's how
Look at what's happening now
Gloom walks intertwined with doom
God's teachings, went out the window
Love, and peace aint in this room
Sodom and Gomorrah
Came to demise, by the same doom
This is some of today's lesson
Find refuge from and evil session
Open the doors, to a blessing
April 5, 2006

Poem Comments/
Interpretation

RIGHT FROM HERE

This isn't a fairy tale
It's bout everyday people
Who watch and still watch
Deflated dream, set sail
It's just matter of fact
Crime on high, and on attack
It's part of the straw
That broke the camel's back
The prayful stopped, they pray less
Here success turns to more stress
The faithful runaway to faith less
The hopeful moved in with the hopeless
This aint what God would teach
Child to future, gun down in the street
Champions of tomorrow, meet defeat
How many times will this story repeat
Love isn't found anywhere
Care's lost, it's not there
Danger lives in the air everywhere
Where do we go, right from here?????????????/
Aug ? 2005

Poem Comments/ Interpretation

_____
_____
_____
_____
_____
_____
_____
_____
_____
_____
_____
_____
_____
_____
_____
_____
_____
_____
_____
_____
_____
_____
_____
_____
_____
_____
_____

Send Your Comments/*Interpretations* to Mr. Larry "Duce" Cobb
email address; roxburypoet@yahoo.com

TO A BRIGHTER DAY

In the beginning
We met, and came together
As birds of a feather
Which bonded us together
In the beginning
We were sharing
Giving and receiving
Praying the other kept living
In the beginning
We laughed to laugh
Two played half and half
Where we became one
So much we have done
In the beginning
There was a cost
Where one was lost
The other was found
Waiting, waiting
For God to make a sound
In the beginning
The truth was heard
Giving through the spoken word
Saying, come this way
From the darkness
To a brighter day
Oct 13, 2004

Poem Comments/ Interpretation

_____

_____

_____

_____

_____

_____

_____

_____

_____

_____

_____

_____

_____

_____

_____

_____

_____

_____

_____

_____

_____

_____

_____

Send Your Comments/Interpretations to Mr. Larry "Duce" Cobb
email address; roxburypoet@yahoo.com

ALL WISH TO KEEP

Where did you
Come from
Was it from where
Honey is made
And the bee's hum
Where the sugar's deep
Within the cone
A sweetness, all wish to keep
2000-2008?

Poem Comments/ Interpretation

_____
_____
_____
_____
_____
_____
_____
_____
_____
_____
_____
_____
_____
_____
_____
_____
_____
_____
_____
_____
_____
_____
_____
_____
_____

Send Your Comments/I_nterpretations_ **to Mr. Larry "Duce" Cobb**
email address; roxburypoet@yahoo.com

LOVING YOU

By God you were sent
An Angel as a present
The giving of
Kindness and care
The receiver of love
Through what we share
We're so different
Yet much the same
That alone makes the difference
Loving you isn't a game
Jan 9, 2002

Poem Comments/ Interpretation

SO THE WORLD

Living in a world
Surrounded by chaos
Love, Hope and Faith
Has a way of getting lost
While good continues to fall
Temptation makes the call
Evil says, welcome to all
Madness and sadness
Are kings and queens of the ball
Righteousness is left behind
Some search for it
Others say, the Hell with it
So the world became unkind
Jan 21, 2008

Poem Comments/ Interpretation

_____
_____
_____
_____
_____
_____
_____
_____
_____
_____
_____
_____
_____
_____
_____
_____
_____
_____
_____
_____
_____
_____
_____
_____
_____
_____
_____

Send Your Comments/Interpretations to Mr. Larry "Duce" Cobb
email address; roxburypoet@yahoo.com

QUENCHED A THIRST

The world lived in today
Aint the same as yesterday
Here the Gospel gone astray
Round the way, where I stay
We lost our own way
I've lived on the dark side
With Satan in front, and God by my side
That place, called the great divide
Where weakness had no room to hide
Every day was a rollercoaster ride
Down for the cause, and the effect
Then the effect straight, from the cause
I ran with the best, of the worst
The crew I rolled with, got down with
Understood one thing only, break the laws
Together just down for the cause
Doing State or County time or Death
Stayed willing to give up all we had left
At that time no questions, just answers
Who in their right mind, aint afraid of Death
Some still here, other's gone in a hearse
Glass of water we drank from, quenched a thirst
April 26, 2006

Poem Comments/
Interpretation

_____
_____
_____
_____
_____
_____
_____
_____
_____
_____
_____
_____
_____
_____
_____
_____
_____
_____
_____
_____
_____
_____
_____
_____
_____
_____

Send Your Comments/Interpretations to Mr. Larry "Duce" Cobb
email address; roxburypoet@yahoo.com

DON'T GO OUT

The game of life
Has no off season
Hear some good advice
It comes with good reason
To some it's not
To other's it's pleasing
Take hold of life
To keep it, keep on squeezing
Watch that hole or grave
Stay tuned, on road you pave
Life not about
Living to be a slave
Many just don't know
Down the river, they go
Lost touch with the flow
Where they're headed
God may only know
Way of life winds upward
Words of God says go forward
My Mama said
Don't go out, of this world backwards
Dec 15, 2005

Poem Comments/ Interpretation

_____
_____
_____
_____
_____
_____
_____
_____
_____
_____
_____
_____
_____
_____
_____
_____
_____
_____
_____
_____
_____
_____
_____
_____
_____
_____

Send Your Comments/Interpretations to Mr. Larry "Duce" Cobb
email address; roxburypoet@yahoo.com

ROXBURY

Roxbury grown
Standing together
Or standing all alone
Between Heaven and Hell
Is the place we roam
However it is, its home
It keeps and keeps on poppin
Like the heat to the corn
Here today, gone tomorrow
The body count aint droppin
Sorry to say, it aint stoppin
Where you stand, many fell
Others living in an upstate cell
Some to many hope they don't
Straight breakdown and tell
About Roxbury grown
Surviving between Heaven and Hell
Aug 20, 2007

Poem Comments/
Interpretation

_____
_____
_____
_____
_____
_____
_____
_____
_____
_____
_____
_____
_____
_____
_____
_____
_____
_____
_____
_____
_____
_____
_____
_____
_____
_____
_____

THIS STORY'S ICE COLD

Is the coast clear
That's some of what
You got to remember
Living round, near here
No one's really safe
Crime leading the race
Aint no hiding place
The front page has no space
Plainview, it's so plain
Unprovoked, gone insane
Defeated wear face of pain
Tears aren't washed by the rain
Many somehow let go
Lost touched with the flow
Down the river they go
Is that someone you know
Missing list grows long
For those who came to belong
Sorry to say, they're gone
A wall stands between
The weak and strong
Where'd we go so, so wrong
Drip, drip, drip another tear
Heart hurts, seeing another bear
On some pole around near here
This picture's seen through the year
Drip, drip, drip another tear
What does the future hold
After what you've been told
About the selling of a soul
Giving it up, to chase some gold
Fact is, This Story's Ice Cold
Sept 16, 2006

Poem Comments/
Interpretation

I WILL NOT BE DENIED

What I have to offer
May be too strong for some
Then there's those
That know what I'm offering must be done
This that I'm speaking of
Has the poisonous strength
That's possessed to the likes
Of a venomous rattle snake
It's hot to the taste
As that of red devil lye
As you see I don't have time to waste
You taste this, you just may die
Because what I'm offering
Has me to the point
As you would be if you drank cyanide
Cause what I must do
I will not be denied
July 14, 1993

Poem Comments/ Interpretation

_____
_____
_____
_____
_____
_____
_____
_____
_____
_____
_____
_____
_____
_____
_____
_____
_____
_____
_____
_____
_____
_____
_____
_____
_____

IT'S JUST RIGHT

Did that hurt
What?
That fall from Heaven
Angels only arrive like you
From beyond the stars
Thank you for passing through
You're what makes a day bright
Whether cloudy, or rainy
The sight of you, it's just right
Date unknown

Poem Comments/
Interpretation

_____
_____
_____
_____
_____
_____
_____
_____
_____
_____
_____
_____
_____
_____
_____
_____
_____
_____
_____
_____
_____
_____
_____
_____

Send Your Comments/Interpretations to Mr. Larry "Duce" Cobb
email address; roxburypoet@yahoo.com

I DON'T KNOW

Just watching the news
It's so, so sad to know
How many mother's, sons and daughters lose
Whether it be the drugs
That lead them
To the hole that's being dug
Or domestic violence
That grew into what became
Death with absolute silence
Was it the gun
That took a mother's
Daughter or maybe even a son
Does anybody know
How to stop
This aimlessly, deadly show
Cause,
I don't know
July 29, 1993

Poem Comments/ Interpretation

GOD'S FOUNTAIN

Through the alley
Below the valley
To the mountain
Drink of God's fountain
The times lived in
Are surrounded by sin
It's hard finding a true friend
Sodom and Gomorrah came to an end
By God, three Angels came
Disappointment, who's the blame
What was, will never be the same
Today's happenings are a crying shame
There is no better time
To search the heart, soul and mind
Only to find the light
With God it's time to get right
Through the alley
Below the valley
To the mountain
Drink of God's fountain..............
March 30, 2008

Poem Comments/ Interpretation

_____
_____
_____
_____
_____
_____
_____
_____
_____
_____
_____
_____
_____
_____
_____
_____
_____
_____
_____
_____
_____
_____
_____
_____
_____
_____

BACK AGAINST THE WALL

Every single step
Of the street
Has its own story
Some shine with hope
Others come up short
Just before, the morning of glory
There's so many chapters
Written within the pages
Of the endless street story
A rising star, rises to fall
Corporate America builds another mall
Saying bring your money big or small
Who cares, who cares
If you're living with your
Back against the wall..............................
March 6, 2008

Poem Comments/ Interpretation

_____
_____
_____
_____
_____
_____
_____
_____
_____
_____
_____
_____
_____
_____
_____
_____
_____
_____
_____
_____
_____
_____
_____

Send Your Comments/Interpretations to Mr. Larry "Duce" Cobb
email address; roxburypoet@yahoo.com

A Distant Mile

The rain continues
To come pouring down
Touching me with thoughts of you
You're here without a sound
My memory serves me well
There it is, your smile
Which comes to me
From a far distant mile
March 16, 2001

Poem Comments/
Interpretation

_____

_____

_____

_____

_____

_____

_____

_____

_____

_____

_____

_____

_____

_____

_____

_____

_____

_____

_____

_____

_____

_____

_____

_____

Above Is Real

My feelings
Continue to climb
Because we've shared
Growth of the mind
You've taken me
To brand new heights
Alone in my bed
You I think of at night
Yes!, this love is a
Many splendid thing
With our love
There's more it shall bring
Because it's
I for you and you for I
We're the ones who make
This thing see eye to eye
Yes! We can make it,
Where others fail
Because we won't
Let our love get stale
That we won't and can't
Let happen between us
Now that ours is built on
Peace, love and trust
With these
We'll travel many miles
Even now, the thought of it
Has made me smile
Sunshine, I can't stop
How I feel
Because all that's written
Above, is real
February 5, 2001

Poem Comments/ Interpretation

_____
_____
_____
_____
_____
_____
_____
_____
_____
_____
_____
_____
_____
_____
_____
_____
_____
_____
_____
_____
_____
_____
_____

Always

You're like
The morning sun
That brings
Joy and fun
You have
Touched me
Now, now
Can't you see
My feelings
Inside
They
No longer hide
With them
I'll share
Because you
Really care
You're one of a kind
Always, you're in my mind....
July 18, 1998

Poem Comments/ Interpretation

Always Be There

You have renewed
What was missing
By the attention
You have been giving
You have become
My ray of hope
When the times
Get hard to cope
Only because you
Really do have care,
All of your qualities
Are unique and rare
To me, all of this
Means so, so much
For us to continue
To stay in touch
May what we've
Come to share
Continue to
Always be there
1998

Poem Comments/ Interpretation

_____
_____
_____
_____
_____
_____
_____
_____
_____
_____
_____
_____
_____
_____
_____
_____
_____
_____
_____
_____
_____
_____
_____
_____
_____
_____

At Work

It seems to me
Within my thoughts
It's your face I see
For me, that's a good thing
Because that gives my heart
More than enough
Reason to sing
All the song of love
These are my thoughts
When it's you
I'm thinking of
Sunshine, while at work
I wrote this one for you
So you'll know just how
Today, I felt about you
February 21, 2001

Poem Comments/ Interpretation

_____
_____
_____
_____
_____
_____
_____
_____
_____
_____
_____
_____
_____
_____
_____
_____
_____
_____
_____
_____
_____
_____
_____
_____
_____
_____

Send Your Comments/Interpretations to Mr. Larry "Duce" Cobb
email address; roxburypoet@yahoo.com

Before We Met

Before we met
Our lives were
Half full
But our hearts touched
You can bet
Now to you
I'm pulled
Nearer and nearer
To me, you come
My dear
February 13, 2001

Poem Comments/ Interpretation

_____
_____
_____
_____
_____
_____
_____
_____
_____
_____
_____
_____
_____
_____
_____
_____
_____
_____
_____
_____
_____
_____
_____
_____
_____
_____

By The Hour

Thoughts of you cross my mind
It seems to happen any time
Whether going about my day
Thinking of the month of May
Holding hands, sitting on the grass
Admiring your pleasingly fat ass
What you don't seem to like, I love
As you see that's what I've been thinking of
But! There's more to you than that
That's why men will tip their hats
Because they know a queen has passed by
When they smile don't ask why
As I, they know
A beautiful blossoming flower
Who is to me
To be loved
By the hour
March 29, 2001

Poem Comments/ Interpretation

_____
_____
_____
_____
_____
_____
_____
_____
_____
_____
_____
_____
_____
_____
_____
_____
_____
_____
_____
_____
_____
_____
_____
_____
_____

Can't Be Wrong

All day long I wait
Through a very long day
Just to hear your voice
And the things you say
Once stranger, but now friends
What we have, let it not end
Friends to lovers, that's strong
What we do, can't be wrong
February 15, 2001

Poem Comments/ Interpretation

_____
_____
_____
_____
_____
_____
_____
_____
_____
_____
_____
_____
_____
_____
_____
_____
_____
_____
_____
_____
_____
_____
_____
_____
_____

Don't Take Away

Through all the travels
Within my every life
Entwined in a sad place
What's meant to be unravels
The coming of a new life
And your smiling face
Your's is a face I respect
After all the love
You've given to me, what's next
Whatever it is, don't take away the love
November 25, 2002

Poem Comments/
Interpretation

Ever Known Before

May good health
And a joyful spirit
Willingly continue
To shine upon you
How have you been?
Will I see you again?
If so will you say when?
We can't let this end
Well as for me
It's you I need to see
Help me find a way
Other than that, I'm ok
I more than understand
The pressures love demands
When it's such a must to hide
The love you need by your side
Thinking of you at times I can't sleep
It's more than a dream of you I want to keep
Cause whenever I wake you're not there
I need the reality of giving you love and care
Through prayer, my hope and a wish
I make one promise and it's this
You'll get love and be loved more
Than anything you've ever known before
October 4, 1998

Poem Comments/ Interpretation

_____
_____
_____
_____
_____
_____
_____
_____
_____
_____
_____
_____
_____
_____
_____
_____
_____
_____
_____
_____
_____
_____
_____
_____

Send Your Comments/Interpretations to Mr. Larry "Duce" Cobb
email address; roxburypoet@yahoo.com

For Us To Keep

Now!! we've come
Beyond knowing
Our joy and fun
Holding the others' hand
Sharing soul soothing laughter
We've grown to understand
Much of what we're after
Kept in our hearts
Throughout the mind
Other's hope, wish to find
Many, many seek
All we hold dear
For us to keep
January 2, 2003

Poem Comments/ Interpretation

_____
_____
_____
_____
_____
_____
_____
_____
_____
_____
_____
_____
_____
_____
_____
_____
_____
_____
_____
_____
_____
_____
_____
_____
_____

Send Your Comments/Interpretations to Mr. Larry "Duce" Cobb
email address; roxburypoet@yahoo.com

From It's Very Start

Another year
Has come and gone
We're still together
Living out and within
The precious, precious lyrics
To an unbelievable love song
You and I know where
Love was forever sent
Whether near or off afar
Togerher we hold many, many
Unforgettable moments
Your love to my heart
My love to you heart
Our loveable love song
Was written from it's very start
January 1, 2003

Poem Comments/ Interpretation

From Me, To You

Come up very close
To receive this toast
For you, being you
From me, to you
If not for you
Who would I give my love to
Yes! You have the ability
To make our love a reality
Because it has grown
Far beyond what we've known
I'm yours and you're mine
It only gets better with time
Because you're the best part
To all the love in my heart
Yes! You've earned the right
To be told this every night
January 26, 2001

Poem Comments/ Interpretation

Send Your Comments/I*nterpretations to Mr. Larry "Duce" Cobb*

email address; roxburypoet@yahoo.com

Good Night

Sunshine! I think of you the most
So! I write this, to send you a toast
By the way, you know what
It's a shear pleasure
Because in you, I know I have
A real treasure
Men! search the world over
For the like of you
So! I'm thanking you
Because I don't have to
Yes! You are all that,
And some
No! My feelings for you
Will never be done
Sunshine! Live with
Your head up high
Because my love for you
I'll never deny
So when you sit in thought
And you're alone
Just remember
My love's in your home
This is only for you to see
And feel the words I write
With that! I say to you
Good Night
February 1, 2001

Poem Comments/ Interpretation

_____
_____
_____
_____
_____
_____
_____
_____
_____
_____
_____
_____
_____
_____
_____
_____
_____
_____
_____
_____
_____
_____
_____
_____

Send Your Comments/Interpretations to Mr. Larry "Duce" Cobb
email address; roxburypoet@yahoo.com

How I Feel

From the minute
That I met you
I knew I had
To be with you
You're the dream
That came true
Because you kept
Coming into my mind
I continued wondering
Would you be mine
To give to you
A love, that's so kind
You took away
All of my loneliness
For you doing that
Here's some happiness
With all of my love
There's no sadness
This love for you
I'll never conceal
I can only show you
That I'm for real
When it's for you
And how I feel
August 27, 1998

Poem Comments/ Interpretation

_____
_____
_____
_____
_____
_____
_____
_____
_____
_____
_____
_____
_____
_____
_____
_____
_____
_____
_____
_____
_____
_____
_____
_____

Send Your Comments/Interpretations to Mr. Larry "Duce" Cobb
email address; roxburypoet@yahoo.com

COME TRUE

I have need to
Just to thank you
For being the lady
That you are
Surely
You're the one
I wished for
When I wished
Upon a star
It was a wish
I never thought
Would come true,
But I was wrong
Now I have you
My wish did
Come true

2001

Poem Comments/ Interpretation

_____
_____
_____
_____
_____
_____
_____
_____
_____
_____
_____
_____
_____
_____
_____
_____
_____
_____
_____
_____
_____
_____
_____
_____
_____
_____
_____

Send Your Comments/Interpretations to Mr. Larry "Duce" Cobb
email address; roxburypoet@yahoo.com

I'll Hold On

The love you share
Has taken me there
Where I need to be
Through your eyes I see
The flickering to a flame
Me loving you I'm to blame
Cause I can't stop the fire
You excite my desire
The feeling's gotten too strong
To have your love, I'll hold on...
1998

Poem Comments/ Interpretation

It's So Sweet

No one seemed to care
That I had love to share
Yeah, I was so all alone
Without a love of my own
Then from heaven you came
Cause of you I'm not the same
My fears you washed them away
I'm stronger today than yesterday
To me, it's you who stand above
That's why to you I give my love
My life, you've given it a lift
It's so sweet, loving a precious gift
1998

Poem Comments/ Interpretation

Send Your Comments/I*nterpretations to Mr. Larry "Duce" Cobb*
email address; roxburypoet@yahoo.com

I've Been Thinking

I've been thinking
About our situation
Love has so many
So many temptations
You can't allow that
To get in the way
If you expect our love
To be here to stay
I understand the pressures
That you're going through
I hope you don't think
It's just happening to you
Sunshine, in my weak moments
You as I must be strong
Now is the moment for us
To do not a thing wrong
This you need to understand
Because this is how I feel
These are meaningful words,
From your man
February 27, 2001

Poem Comments/ Interpretation

Let The Whole World See

Through life all wonder
Where will it go
As the situation
We've come to know
Even with our distance
We'll never part
We've done what others don't
We've bared our hearts
Once we were strangers
But now we're friends
Something out this story
Should never ever end
Because with it came
A care many don't see
We've grown to understand
What's between you and me
Like all the feelings
You and I kept inside
What's so important
Nothing to the other, do we hide
For us getting together
May be a wait
We can't let nothing stop
The love we cultivate
As you see it's grown
Beyond belief, let it grow
You're the water to quench
My thirst, don't you know
Your top secret
Means so much to me
Showing care for you
I'd let the whole world see
January 28, 2001

Poem Comments/ Interpretation

Lovable

What's written it's true
When it comes to you
It's something I know
Even if you don't think so
Knowing you, it's wonderful
Because you're beautiful
To me you're adorable
And you're more than lovable
1998

Poem Comments/ Interpretation

Love and Care

By way of heaven
To me, you were sent
With a loveable heart
Thinking of you, I smile
The happiness you bring
To share yours with me
You're beyond compare
You leave me no choice
But to give to you
Love and care
1998

Poem Comments/ Interpretation

Love of Tomorrow

Without you here
I hear your voice
Through my listening
I look to see your face
Then I begin to search
My memories to find you
Then there you are
Wearing that caring smile
From that, sitting here
I feel your warmth
Which has traveled miles
To touch me
At times, no all the time
I'm at the center of your heart
Not just wanting to be
Between your precious thighs
But I won't leave that
Out and that's for sure
Without you here
My heart knows you're near
As you see, you're here
Even though you're there
These are some of my thoughts for today
With our love of tomorrow
Let's keep it like yesterday
March 4, 2001

Poem Comments/ Interpretation

Love To Share

Within my heart
You have a place
So that your heart
Will always be safe
There I have for you
Respect, love and care
This and more for you
Because you had love to share
1998

Poem Comments/ Interpretation

_____
_____
_____
_____
_____
_____
_____
_____
_____
_____
_____
_____
_____
_____
_____
_____
_____
_____
_____
_____
_____
_____
_____
_____

Send Your Comments/Interpretations to Mr. Larry "Duce" Cobb
email address; roxburypoet@yahoo.com

My Eyes

My nature comes alive
Right from the very minute
You come before my eyes
You have a spell
That works on me
Oh so very well
For me this is it
That makes me offer you
A feeling that will never quit
Yes! This has been going on
For quite some time
The power of this love,
Has gotten strong
This can't stop
Because you life my nature up,
To where it can't stop
My nature comes alive
Right from the very minute
You come before my eyes
January 31, 2001

Poem Comments/
Interpretation

My Friend

Thank you my friend
For allowing me in
To see your other side
The person you hide
It's a beauty to see
What others can't be
You opened your treasure chest
To see your care, you're the best
By doing that, you've lifted me up
From the quicksand, I'm no longer stuck
With my pencil to you I write
That's something I do every night
You wouldn't believe just how many
Put it to you like this, it's plenty
To the point something's grown
With your friendship I'm not alone
Whenever you're feeling down
Quietly sit than hear the sound
Listen and feel the wind
I'm that close to you my friend...
July 30, 1998

Poem Comments/ Interpretation

_____
_____
_____
_____
_____
_____
_____
_____
_____
_____
_____
_____
_____
_____
_____
_____
_____
_____
_____
_____
_____
_____

Send Your Comments/_Interpretations_ to Mr. Larry "_Duce_" _Cobb_
email address; roxburypoet@yahoo.com

My Girl

Another day has come
With thoughts of you
Working with these thoughts
I'm finding it's hard to do
That happens to men
All around the world
When they, as I, remember
The smile of my girl
Date unknown

Poem Comments/
Interpretation

_____

_____

_____

_____

_____

_____

_____

_____

_____

_____

_____

_____

_____

_____

_____

_____

_____

_____

_____

_____

_____

_____

_____

_____

_____

Send Your Comments/Interpretations to Mr. Larry "Duce" Cobb
email address; roxburypoet@yahoo.com

My Sunshine

Last night, sometime
I attempted to sleep
But into my mind
You continued to creep
Closer and closer you came
From my meeting with you
I'll never be the same
Because I couldn't keep you
You're there, then gone
I know in my heart
We're the lyrics to a love song
And you're the best part
Because lady, seems you
Stay on my mind
Thoughts of you
Are my sunshine
July 16, 1998

Poem Comments/
Interpretation

Nights and Days

Imagine with me
What's written, hope you see
Awaking, middle of night
Warmth I feel you to my right
I extend my hand
You meet me, all because
You are the one who understands
Along our life's pathways
Somehow or another
Unbeknownst to us
We would brighten the others'
Many, many night and days
November 24, 2002

Poem Comments/ Interpretation

No More

What makes you
So, so special for me
Your loyalty
And your honesty
All my life
What you have and give
Is what I've searched for
With the gift from God, you
I thank him
I search no more
November 24, 2002

Poem Comments/
Interpretation

On The Train

I'm on the train again
Sitting and riding with
Thoughts of
My most precious
And closest friend
I wear a smile
Thinking of your face
As I move about
Wherever I'm at
For my place
That's the kind of spell
You have on me
The spell of peace,
Joy, love, happiness
Those are the things
You've added
To my life
Now I'm getting off
The train again
Just thinking
Of you
My closest friend
March 9, 2001

Poem Comments/
Interpretation

_____
_____
_____
_____
_____
_____
_____
_____
_____
_____
_____
_____
_____
_____
_____
_____
_____
_____
_____
_____
_____
_____
_____
_____
_____

Our Hearts

Now life's not
A lonely life to live
With all the love
You have to give
Others can only hope
And dream of this
Having a love
That's more than a promise
Being away from you
I feel you so near
Absence makes our love
Stronger my dear
Only because ours
Is never far apart
The love we possess
It's kept in our hearts
2001

Poem Comments/
Interpretation

_____
_____
_____
_____
_____
_____
_____
_____
_____
_____
_____
_____
_____
_____
_____
_____
_____
_____
_____
_____
_____
_____
_____
_____

Send Your Comments/Interpretations to Mr. Larry "Duce" Cobb
email address; roxburypoet@yahoo.com

Our Love

Our love
Has been built
With care in mind
Our love
Has stood for
Good reason, sunshine
We're doing
What other don't do
Like keeping our love true
January 10, 2001

Poem Comments/
Interpretation

_____
_____
_____
_____
_____
_____
_____
_____
_____
_____
_____
_____
_____
_____
_____
_____
_____
_____
_____
_____
_____
_____
_____

Send Your Comments/Interpretations to Mr. Larry "Duce" Cobb
email address; roxburypoet@yahoo.com

Paths

Every day's special
For you
Every day's special
For me
Because our
Paths came across
December 3, 2002

Poem Comments/ Interpretation

Put It There

Within the heart
We've come together
To never part
There's nothing wrong
With you and I
Sharing love so strong
The smile I wear
Comes from you
You, put it there
1998

Poem Comments/
Interpretation

_____

_____

_____

_____

_____

_____

_____

_____

_____

_____

_____

_____

_____

_____

_____

_____

_____

_____

_____

_____

_____

_____

_____

_____

Send Your Comments/Interpretations to Mr. Larry "Duce" Cobb
email address; roxburypoet@yahoo.com

Question

While sitting by the phone
Thinking of the question
You brought to my attention
On that, there's much to mention
Because you do have
Plenty of care
That's why I give you
My love to share
By the way
I don't think
That's a question
You have to ask,
Not me
But I understand
Why you ask
Baby, it's not good
To question
A love that feels
Good
2001

Poem Comments/
Interpretation

_____
_____
_____
_____
_____
_____
_____
_____
_____
_____
_____
_____
_____
_____
_____
_____
_____
_____
_____
_____
_____
_____
_____
_____
_____
_____
_____
_____
_____

Send Your Comments/Interpretations to Mr. Larry "Duce" Cobb
email address; roxburypoet@yahoo.com

Sending This

I'm sending this
On the wings of a dove
With hopes it doesn't drop
That package contains my love
But if it does, I wish
It would land in peace
So that the understanding
For our love will increase
Beyond those who've lost
What we wish to keep
Here's my inner most thoughts
Though my dream while I sleep
February 16, 2001

Poem Comments/ Interpretation

Sharing

Sugar, my days are spent
With thoughts of you
The one who's heaven sent
What did I do
To deserve this
Meeting with you
Never, ever is it through
We have what
The other's are after
Here is that, what!!!
Sharing the joys of laughter
November 24, 2002

Poem Comments/ Interpretation

_____
_____
_____
_____
_____
_____
_____
_____
_____
_____
_____
_____
_____
_____
_____
_____
_____
_____
_____
_____
_____
_____
_____
_____
_____
_____
_____

Send Your Comments/_Interpretations_ to Mr. Larry "Duce" Cobb
email address; roxburypoet@yahoo.com

Sitting Here

Sitting here looking
Out my window
I'm having thoughts
You should know
Thinking what we
Have is a dream
If it is that would
Be cold and mean
Because it's a dream
I wish to keep
Even after I've awakened
From a sleep
I never thought
I'd be touched like this
Walking through my day
You're the one I miss
Because of the love
And care you give
Giving me more reason
To keep our love
Alive to live
March 10, 2001

Poem Comments/ Interpretation

_____

_____
_____
_____
_____
_____
_____
_____
_____
_____
_____
_____
_____
_____
_____
_____
_____
_____
_____
_____
_____
_____
_____

Send Your Comments/*Interpretations* to Mr. Larry "Duce" Cobb
email address; roxburypoet@yahoo.com

Something Bright

To me, you're the light
That turned my life
From dark, to something bright
While all the time
Having a heart, and soul
That's worth to me, more than gold
Yes! It's a pleasure
To know and love
Such a precious treasure
January 27, 2001

Poem Comments/ Interpretation

Springtime

Springtime has come
Upon our lives
With it's coming
Comes so many thoughts
To cultivating the love
We've sought
Through the long
Cold winters chill
Giving us feelings of
A midsummer breeze
Can you feel the warmth
Of my hand touching you
All over
That's something I plan to do
Because it's something
I love to do
Touching you
March 26, 2001

Poem Comments/ Interpretation

That Saturday

Sunshine, I'm sitting here
Thinking of you my dear
With a longing to be with you
To share what we're going through
By no means, do we need mistakes
For our love,
We're playing for higher stakes
Each and every night
Before I go to sleep
I pray we hold on
To the love, we wish to keep
Because what we share
To me, means so much
Writing this now
I can feel your touch
Since that Saturday
Our love has been reborn
It's grown to new heights
And surely a ways beyond
Anything that I've ever
Possessed before
By the way, I surely
Want and need more
Of your love, because
To me it feels so good
We have what others
Others would if they could
So let's not let our strong
Feelings get in the way
Then we'll continue to hold hands
As we did that Saturday
March 3, 2001

Poem Comments/ Interpretation

_____
_____
_____
_____
_____
_____
_____
_____
_____
_____
_____
_____
_____
_____
_____
_____
_____
_____
_____
_____
_____
_____
_____
_____
_____

Send Your Comments/Interpretations to Mr. Larry "Duce" Cobb
email address; roxburypoet@yahoo.com

That You Took

In grounds I see
Your fear
Everywhere I go
Just about any place
With just one look
It was my eyes
That you
took
February 22, 2001

Poem Comments/
Interpretation

_____
_____
_____
_____
_____
_____
_____
_____
_____
_____
_____
_____
_____
_____
_____
_____
_____
_____
_____
_____
_____
_____
_____
_____

The Angel

Beyond my dreams
You came
Bearing gifts
Of
Joy, laughter and happiness
To God I thank
For to me
The angel he sent
You
December 3, 2002

Poem Comments/ Interpretation

_____
_____
_____
_____
_____
_____
_____
_____
_____
_____
_____
_____
_____
_____
_____
_____
_____
_____
_____
_____
_____
_____
_____
_____
_____

Send Your Comments/Interpretations to Mr. Larry "Duce" Cobb
email address; roxburypoet@yahoo.com

The Best

People only dream
About what we have
And share
Because most don't have
Hearts filled with care
So that makes us different
From all the rest
Because we possess
A love that's the best
January 31, 2001

Poem Comments/ Interpretation

_____
_____
_____
_____
_____
_____
_____
_____
_____
_____
_____
_____
_____
_____
_____
_____
_____
_____
_____
_____
_____
_____
_____
_____
_____
_____
_____

The Best Parts

My whole body does shake
From all of the nakedness
Which my mind seems to make
I'm not alone, you're there
Because together
We share so much love and care
Before the other
We stand, eye to eye
Face to face
Traveling to that place
We unlock the door
We're there in the others heart
Mind, body, love and more
We're givers and receivers
Of the best parts
November 25, 2002

Poem Comments/ Interpretation

_____
_____
_____
_____
_____
_____
_____
_____
_____
_____
_____
_____
_____
_____
_____
_____
_____
_____
_____
_____
_____
_____
_____
_____

Send Your Comments/Interpretations to Mr. Larry "Duce" Cobb
email address; roxburypoet@yahoo.com

The Dove

Out of many others' dreams
We came to be
Have no shame
What others' can't see
For us, was Cupid's aim
The aim was
For us to live within our love
Give what was
And is carried by the dove
November 24, 2002

Poem Comments/ Interpretation

_____
_____
_____
_____
_____
_____
_____
_____
_____
_____
_____
_____
_____
_____
_____
_____
_____
_____
_____
_____
_____
_____
_____

Send Your Comments/Interpretations to Mr. Larry "Duce" Cobb
email address; roxburypoet@yahoo.com

Through My Window

Through my window
The sun shines
But! That's not the one
That's been on my mind
There's only one, just one
That I consider my sunshine
She's loveable and filled with fun
Writing about you I'm never done
Because from a dream she came
To my heart from Cupid's aim
Yes, I accept all of your love
That was granted to me from above
February 1, 2001

Poem Comments/ Interpretation

_____
_____
_____
_____
_____
_____
_____
_____
_____
_____
_____
_____
_____
_____
_____
_____
_____
_____
_____
_____
_____
_____
_____
_____
_____

Send Your Comments/Interpretations to Mr. Larry "Duce" Cobb
email address; roxburypoet@yahoo.com

Time and Place

To you, I must say
Your presence
Has touched me
With a thrill
That won't go away
On the train
This morning, I felt you
But the sad part is
I couldn't reach you
Sitting there
I went to touch your face
I was thinking
Of another, time and place
February 19, 2001

Poem Comments/ Interpretation

_____
_____
_____
_____
_____
_____
_____
_____
_____
_____
_____
_____
_____
_____
_____
_____
_____
_____
_____
_____
_____
_____
_____
_____

To Be Continued

The forest
You and I
A rock
Hands touch skin
Just us
A friend
You trust
Middle of winter
Between us
Heat hot as summer
To be continued....
December 3, 2002

Poem Comments/ Interpretation

_____
_____
_____
_____
_____
_____
_____
_____
_____
_____
_____
_____
_____
_____
_____
_____
_____
_____
_____
_____
_____
_____
_____

Send Your Comments/Interpretations to Mr. Larry "Duce" Cobb
email address; roxburypoet@yahoo.com

To Be Wonderful

Destiny's brought us together
Who are we to question
The powers of love
Put us so close together
Distance can't stop us
Because what you have in me
I have in you, that I trust
Here it is again....destiny
Our beginning
Was beautiful
Now it's beginning
To be wonderful
November 24, 2002

Poem Comments/
Interpretation

_____
_____
_____
_____
_____
_____
_____
_____
_____
_____
_____
_____
_____
_____
_____
_____
_____
_____
_____
_____
_____
_____
_____

To Feel Your Touch

Hello there Sunshine
May good health and spirits
Be your's all the time
Cause its important for me
To know and understand
You're as important for me
To know and understand
You're as well as you can be
Because I've grown to care
So very much about you
And the special things we share
Yes! You're very special to me
Cause you've touched my heart
This love's just meant to be
Your heart's safe in my hand
It will be protected and respected
Sunshine! This you must understand
This is just the way I feel

You're good for me, I'm good for you
Believe this, what's written in so real
I'm the warmth when you are cold
Cause the loving and love I'll give you
Will touch heart, mind, body and soul
Sit down relax a moment
Because you need to know
To me, you were heaven sent
From the lyrics to a song
Heaven's missing an angel
But now, to me you belong
No! My love won't go away
Because it's all of yours
Wherever you're at, it will stay
Show me your love's for real
My needs have gotten stronger
Come to me to tell me how you feel
All over, I want to touch you
Am I wrong wanting you so much
Say I'm right needing to feel you touch ..September
15, 1998

Poem Comments/
Interpretation

_____
_____
_____
_____
_____
_____
_____
_____
_____
_____
_____
_____
_____
_____
_____
_____
_____
_____
_____
_____
_____
_____
_____
_____

Send Your Comments/Interpretations to Mr. Larry "Duce" Cobb
email address; roxburypoet@yahoo.com

To Keep

Like the ocean
My love for you
Runs so very deep
Something I want
All that I need
Is your love, to keep
1998

Poem Comments/ Interpretation

_____
_____
_____
_____
_____
_____
_____
_____
_____
_____
_____
_____
_____
_____
_____
_____
_____
_____
_____
_____
_____
_____
_____
_____
_____
_____
_____
_____
_____

Send Your Comments/Interpretations to Mr. Larry "Duce" Cobb
email address; roxburypoet@yahoo.com

To Us

What we share, is a must
Things we hold
Are kept just for us
Allow memories to serve you well
As your daily thoughts travel
To your wishing, wishing well
Holiday season's upon us
A gift's just a gift to the other
We're presents to us
December 9, 2002

Poem Comments/ Interpretation

_____
_____
_____
_____
_____
_____
_____
_____
_____
_____
_____
_____
_____
_____
_____
_____
_____
_____
_____
_____
_____
_____
_____
_____
_____
_____
_____
_____
_____

Send Your Comments/Interpretations to Mr. Larry "Duce" Cobb
email address; roxburypoet@yahoo.com

WE CAN TRUST

I miss you more
Far more than before
For you these feelings
Keep my heart reeling
What I have for you
Let these words touch you
Yes! Every part of me
It's for your eyes to see
How did we get to this
Missing something, we miss
No, no questions as to why
Heart's have no reason to lie
Our paths led us
To us
Surely our hearts
We can trust
February 5, 2001

Poem Comments/ Interpretation

Touch You

You must understand
Beside you, I stand
How can I not be
When you're there for me
So put your worries aside
My love for you won't hide
Something my love can and will do
All over, it will touch you
1998

Poem Comments/ Interpretation

_____
_____
_____
_____
_____
_____
_____
_____
_____
_____
_____
_____
_____
_____
_____
_____
_____
_____
_____
_____
_____
_____
_____
_____
_____

Send Your Comments/_Interpretations to **Mr. Larry "Duce" Cobb**_
email address; roxburypoet@yahoo.com

Trust

Sugar, whatever
Brought us
To this place
And this time
It had to be
Built on trust
Through sharing
Our hearts and our minds
We're the ones
To blame
For cupids'
Tremendous aim
March 1, 2001

Poem Comments/
Interpretation

_____
_____
_____
_____
_____
_____
_____
_____
_____
_____
_____
_____
_____
_____
_____
_____
_____
_____
_____
_____
_____
_____

Send Your Comments/Interpretations to Mr. Larry "Duce" Cobb
email address; roxburypoet@yahoo.com

What We Have

What we have
To many may be strange
What we have
May it never change
What we have
It's meant to be
What we have
Belongs to you and me
March 29, 2001

Poem Comments/ Interpretation

_____
_____
_____
_____
_____
_____
_____
_____
_____
_____
_____
_____
_____
_____
_____
_____
_____
_____
_____
_____
_____
_____
_____
_____

Send Your Comments/*Interpretations to Mr. Larry "Duce" Cobb*
email address; roxburypoet@yahoo.com

With Mines

Since knowing you
Much joy I've gone through
Time and time again
You've shown, you're a true friend
That alone shows I'm blessed
Since knowing you
I've touched much happiness
You're a God given gift
Whose heart's warm and kind
I'm thankful you share
All your love with mines
November 25, 2002

Poem Comments/ Interpretation

_____
_____
_____
_____
_____
_____
_____
_____
_____
_____
_____
_____
_____
_____
_____
_____
_____
_____
_____
_____
_____
_____
_____
_____

Send Your Comments/Interpretations to Mr. Larry "Duce" Cobb
email address; roxburypoet@yahoo.com

With The Love I Bring

I do understand the pain
Which runs through your brain
But hate is conquered by love
With the olive branch carried by the dove
Which possesses the love I have for you
To help with the time you're going through
Allow me to remind you you're not alone
Because your pain, yes is my own
When you suffer, I suffer as well
This is something to you, I must tell
What you'll read, comes from the heart
I've loved you from the very start
The day you waved from the window
Then it was you I wanted to know
Not because of prison, I felt your need
To be released, so I just took heed
Being caged your heart won't sing
Now your heart's opened
With the love I bring
March 23, 2001

Poem Comments/
Interpretation

_____
_____
_____
_____
_____
_____
_____
_____
_____
_____
_____
_____
_____
_____
_____
_____
_____
_____
_____
_____
_____
_____
_____
_____
_____
_____
_____

Send Your Comments/Interpretations to Mr. Larry "Duce" Cobb
email address; roxburypoet@yahoo.com

Won't Run Out

Here's something you
Mustn't think about
Not ever
My love
Won't run pout
On you, not ever
For you, I have it
In abundance
Wherever you're at
Or whatever the distance
February 12, 2001

Poem Comments/ Interpretation

_____
_____
_____
_____
_____
_____
_____
_____
_____
_____
_____
_____
_____
_____
_____
_____
_____
_____
_____
_____
_____
_____
_____
_____
_____
_____
_____

Send Your Comments/_Interpretations to Mr. Larry "Duce" Cobb_
email address; roxburypoet@yahoo.com

Written With The Love

From what you'll read
You'll see where
My thoughts will lead
So with me, show a smile
As you read
This awhile
You've shown me
The better part
Right from the start
By opening your heart
Only to offer me in
As your lover
But more importantly
As your friend
You possess a quality
That shows me
You're to be loved
That to me is a reality
What you see is a sign
That my love for you
Will last a lifetime
For you, I'll do this for
But if there's a need
Surely I'll do more
Written with the love
Of touching you
By a man that truly
Does love you
February 4, 2001

Poem Comments/ Interpretation

_____
_____
_____
_____
_____
_____
_____
_____
_____
_____
_____
_____
_____
_____
_____
_____
_____
_____
_____
_____
_____
_____
_____
_____
_____
_____

Send Your Comments/_Interpretations_ to Mr. Larry "Duce" Cobb
email address; roxburypoet@yahoo.com

Yesterday

This is so true
Me not seeing you
It's just like this
You're the one I miss
If there
Was a way
I'd been there
Some time yesterday
1998

Poem Comments/ Interpretation

_____
_____
_____
_____
_____
_____
_____
_____
_____
_____
_____
_____
_____
_____
_____
_____
_____
_____
_____
_____
_____
_____
_____
_____
_____
_____
_____
_____

Send Your Comments/Interpretations *to Mr. Larry "Duce" Cobb*
email address; roxburypoet@yahoo.com

COMES BACK TO ME

Here's something important
That can't never
To you, I must say
Be taken away
All about my feelings
Not the joys and thrills
Of yesterday
We shared yesterday
Preparing for our date
With the time we put in
3 years was worth the wait
For my lady friend
You're the one love
That I once set free
The lovable caring dove
Who now, comes back to me
February 18, 2001

Poem Comments/ Interpretation

PRECIOUS TREASURE

You and me
I for you
Ours is a love
That will never be through
Because it's
Meant to last
It was cultivated
By and through our past
I never thought
It would come about
Yesterday removed
Any and all my doubts
On the train platform
You I couldn't see
Then low and behold
You were beside me
Yes! Together
Walking, holding hands
A look, a chuckle, a laugh
All in all still holding hands
My! My! My! That is
A beautiful picture
Hanging in my memory
As a precious treasure

Poem Comments/ Interpretation

_____
_____
_____
_____
_____
_____
_____
_____
_____
_____
_____
_____
_____
_____
_____
_____
_____
_____
_____
_____
_____
_____
_____
_____

Send Your Comments/_Interpretations_ **to Mr. Larry "Duce" Cobb**
email address; roxburypoet@yahoo.com

You've Continued

You've continued
To always be
So, so much
And more to me
You've continued
Being my hope
When life for me
Gets so hard to cope
You've continued
To get all my love
I'm thankful to God
For sending you, for me to love
1998

Poem Comments/
Interpretation

_____
_____
_____
_____
_____
_____
_____
_____
_____
_____
_____
_____
_____
_____
_____
_____
_____
_____
_____
_____
_____
_____

Send Your Comments/Interpretations to Mr. Larry "Duce" Cobb
email address; roxburypoet@yahoo.com

Heartfelt, amazing and sincere......A must read.
Mr. Joseph C. Crawford

A book of poetry that's parallel to the life and times of many. I sincerely urge all to read and collaborate with the author Mr. Cobb.
Mr. Andrew (YIE) Roberts